NASTY WOMEN
TALK BACK

Feminist essays on the global women's marches

Edited by
Joy Watson & Amanda Gouws
with essays from 28 feminist contributors

Imbali
ACADEMIC PUBLISHERS

First published 2018

Imbali Academic Publishers
31 Lympleigh Road, Plumstead, 7801, Cape Town, South Africa
www.imbaliacademic.co.za

© In compilation: Amanda Gouws, Joy Watson
© In illustrations, excluding cover and part page art: Adam Carnegie

ISBN (print) 978-0-6399636-0-0
ISBN (ePUB) 978-0-6399636-1-7

Copy editing: Jenn Warren
Proofreading: Lindy-Joy Dennis
Cover and part page art: Kate True
Cover design: Collaboration Corporation
Illustration and design: Adam Carnegie
Typesetting: Lebone Publishing Services

Printed in South Africa by Novus Print Solutions

CONTENTS

PREFACE

Nasty Women Talk Back is a labour of love that took some time from its inception to completion, since both editors hold full-time jobs that are quite demanding.

As the editors of *Nasty Women Talk Back* we were quite delighted when Imbali Academic Publishers agreed to publish our book, a group of dynamic women who made the publishing process a very special one. Yet, after finding a publisher, we faced another challenge – the use of the Women's Marches posters as they appeared online. With the use of online material copyright issues can become quite challenging. We would have had to get the permission from every person who appeared in the photos taken during the Women's Marches. Even if we wanted to, it would have been impossible. Publishing the essays without the visual material was not an option. We then decided that the online posters from the Women's Marches would form the basis for the illustrations that appear in this book.

Our very talented and imaginative illustrator, Adam Carnegie, read each essay carefully and made a fitting illustration that captured the essence of the online posters. He also did this in a very short period of time and under immense deadline pressure. We cannot thank him enough for his time and commitment to make this book a success. Without his generosity, this book would have taken longer to see the light. Adam worked from a process of reading, absorbing and trying to get a feel for the essays. In so doing, he was reflexive and deeply conscious of his own gendered identity and the ways in which this manifested in his art. This sensitivity shines through in the illustrations and we have ended up with artwork that adds an additional layer to these very thought provoking essays.

The illustrations, in a sense, capture more than the posters because they engage with the text – something that the posters could not do. It also opens new interpretations through a feminist gaze on the Women's Marches. The thought that went into the illustrations become the visual conduit through which we launch into the narrative, with the words and visuals working in tandem to get us to think about feminist lived realities.

We also thank Kate True, a contributor to this collection, who created the artwork for the book's cover. Kate is a gifted painter, portrait artist and curator. As a feminist, she instinctively knew what we wanted, and breathed life into an image that captured the "feeling" of the book.

We hope that you will enjoy both the words and images in this very special collection – it has been the product of so much artistic reflection.

Joy and Amanda

INTRODUCTION

It started as a conversation amongst three feminist friends while we were doing a "women thing" – baking cookies on a rainy afternoon in Cape Town. There was also wine involved – not in the cookies, but in our glasses. We were disgusted that Donald Trump was elected as President of the United States of America (USA). We were mortified by the loss of the opportunity to have the first woman President in the White House. That Hillary Clinton lost to a man like Donald Trump added insult to injury.

But here we were in Cape Town, not the USA, feeling as though we had a personal stake in Hillary's loss. The presidential campaign in the USA grabbed the global imagination. It also grabbed the feminist imagination, presenting the hope that if Hillary could become President of the USA, if after 227 years the USA would finally have its first woman President, women would finally break through that reinforced glass ceiling. It was not to be. There are those who argue that Hillary Clinton herself was the problem, that her own personal and political past did not make her the most likeable candidate (as though Trump's past made him a very likeable candidate!). Women are always more closely scrutinised for the top job, for any position of power. But this is beside the point. What Hillary represented was the hope of many feminists, that women have finally arrived in the last bastion of male power.

Hillary's loss was more than a lost opportunity. It was the metaphorical kick in the feminist gut on a global scale. How was it possible that a misogynist who boasts about grabbing women's pussies became President of the USA on the back of so many women's votes? The discourse that emanated from Trump's tweets, from his vulgar display of misogyny against Hillary Clinton during the presidential debates, to the pussy grabbing video and threats of the immediate rollback of many gains women have made through the hard slog and feminist activism in the trenches. All these efforts were thrown in our faces when election results were announced on 9 November 2016. From the feminist community worldwide arose a deep mourning.

It was the name calling that really smarted – "Nasty Women." Trump called ("crooked") Hillary a Nasty Woman, and by doing so, he called all of us who stand up for women's humanity and women's rights "Nasty Women." First we were angry, and then it felt empowering to embrace the label of "Nasty Women." Isn't that what women who talk back to patriarchy are always called? Nasty!

We were inspired by the Women's Marches all over the world. Women also marched in our city, in Cape Town. Back in the kitchen, Raenette talked about the posters in the Marches – how there were so many pictures and slogans, and how they set her thinking. We discussed the ones that grabbed our attention, and an idea was born – let's write about this! Let's get feminists on board to write our own interpretations of the posters! Let's use the Women's Marches and the way in which it galvanised us into action, to put pen to paper and show fervour for ongoing feminist activism! We ate cookies, drank wine and got very excited. Maybe it was time that we showed the world what Nasty Women are capable of when they pick up pens!

The voices in this book speak from a deeply personal place about how this moment in history – the Donald Trump/Hillary Clinton moment – led us to introspection about what was lost during the 2016 US election for women, but specifically for women who live as feminists.

We were not the only women who felt we had to say something about this moment in history. Another collection, titled *Nasty Women* (Picador, 2017), appeared on the shelves. It is also a collection of essays written by women in the aftermath of Trump's election, speaking to the implications of the loss in the USA and for places elsewhere in the world. We were happy to see this in the bookstores, and we want more and more women to speak out – to mark this moment as one of resistance.

We approached women from across the globe, women with whom we have lifelong networks, women who have inspired us through their writing, women who we knew had something profound to say. The voices are global in scope, but rooted in women's lived experiences of being feminists in specific local contexts. Those who live in the Global

North have a more up close and personal view of Trump, while others share from the geographical distance situating us in the Global South. But regardless of where these feminists call home, none of us are out of reach of neo-liberal globalisation and its exports.

The wide range of posters selected by the contributors speak to our own personal observations and location in the world, the ripple effect of Trump's election, and the pervasive impact of partriarchy. And while the collection brings together a range of different voices in different spaces, from different contextual realities, these essays all speak to a story of how we are living our feminism in ways that contribute towards social change. This was very important to us – to tell narratives that link our personal stories with deeply political issues. The 25 essays and three poems in this collection are all written by Nasty Women who make the personal political; who seek to live their lives in ways that resist and challenge patriarchy. These are stories that speak to the creation of a different kind of social order – one based on equity, the promotion of human rights and social justice.

For each of us, books hold tremendous power and we have a deep respect for the power of the ideas that emanate from them. Each of us has been influenced by the words of feminist writers who have shaped and framed our ways of thinking. Long after we absorb the words and put the books down, the ideas linger on. So in turn, we hope that some of the words and experiences shared in this collection will leap off the page, resonate with you and become an undercurrent that flows with you in your own journeys of feminism, resistance, activism and creating a better world.

Joy Watson, Amanda Gouws and Raenette Gottardo

Note on terminology

The use of the term "womxn" became prominent during the Women's Marches as well as the #FeesMustFall in South Africa. It is a feminist spelling of women – to exclude the use of "men" in wo-men. It also refers to feminist intersectionality and greater inclusivity of people that are gender non-conforming. Womyn is the term that was used by Radical Feminist of the 70's and 80's. Some authors in the book use womxn depending on the context they refer to, other authors use women.

The term "cis gender" or "cisgender" is the association with the sex that someone was assigned at birth. Therefore, if you are born a woman and you accept that designation, you are a cis woman.

FEMINISM AND THE POLITICAL

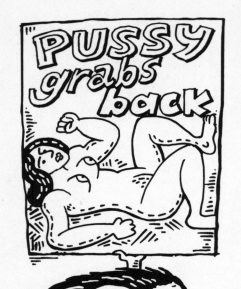

PUSSIES ARE NOT FOR GRABBING!

Joy Watson

I was nine years old when I first experienced pussy grabbing. I was feeling unwell, had been vomiting and, with a high fever, was lethargic and out of sorts. My mother took me to see a white doctor in an established part of Cape Town's Southern Suburbs. For a reason that I cannot recall, I went into the doctor's surgery alone for the examination while my mother waited in the reception area. She was called in afterwards for the diagnosis. I remember lying on the doctor's bed, waiting patiently to get back home where I could be sick in peace. After doing the usual sort of thing, such as listening to my heartbeat and looking inside my mouth, the doctor explained that he would need to examine every part of me. He slid my panties aside and inserted his fingers into my vagina, gently probing around for a bit. I remember the sense of blindly trusting in his established authority. I had no reason to believe that anything untoward had happened. I thought that he was just doing his job and looking for viruses. In my childhood innocence, everything was perfectly as it should be.

Ten years later, still wrapped in my cloak of innocence and blind belief that nice white doctors could not possibly engage in acts of sexual violence, I went to see a gynaecologist. I was 18, a student at the University of Cape Town, and in desperate need of resolving the misery of thrush that had established itself in my nether parts. At the time, I had no idea what thrush was (blame *apartheid* education ...) and had contorted all sorts of dire explanations for what could possibly be wrong. Suffice it to say, I am adept at conjuring up stories of doom, gloom and imminent death. These were the days before the internet, when Catholic school "guidance" programmes did very little in the way of preparing you for the practicalities of understanding your body and sexuality. Our sex education classes were crisp and clear and, in a nutshell, amounted to "total abstinence until marriage, at which point you get to wear a white dress and veil." This, of course, did not provide me with any contextual information to help me understand the intricacies of thrush.

So off I went to the rooms of a gynaecologist in Sea Point, a respected man whose clientele included many affluent women. I know this because he deemed it necessary to tell me. After a somewhat lengthy "chat" at his desk where he asked me many personal questions, he told me to undress in an adjoining room and to get up onto the examination bed while he waited at his desk. He said he would join me in a bit. I took off my clothes and lay there, worried about the foul business going on in my vagina and hoping that he would not be put off. Luckily, the doctor seemed non-plussed and chatted merrily away while examining my breasts and doing a pap smear. With an approving eye, he told me that I had a nice body and asked how I managed to keep it in such good shape. While I had a sense that there was something about him that I did not like, possibly the fact that he seemed so cocky and self-assured, I trusted him completely, trapped by both of our cognitive views of the skewed power relations between us.

When he was done, he told me to get dressed and to join him at his desk. He left the room and I felt tremendous relief that the business of having a strange man poke around in my vagina was done with. I had not been given a dressing gown, so I took my naked self off the examination bed and walked towards the part of the room where my clothes lay in a heap. I was halfway across the room when the door opened and the doctor came back with a "Sorry, sorry, I forgot to check something." I stood there, shy and awkward, trying to cover myself with my arms, rendered vulnerable and exposed. He told me to get back onto the examination bed. I clamoured back on, feeling mortified. It did not cross my mind that I could query this sudden about-turn of events. Muttering about needing to check something, the doctor stepped towards me and, without gloves, proceeded to probe me with his fingers, looking inside my vagina. He told me that he thought that I was possibly anaemic and that it worried him, because I was a "waif of a water nymph." Something about it felt wrong, but I was far too trusting to think that he had any ulterior motives. Also, I had no idea what a water nymph was, which was the main dilemma that I chose to focus on. I dismissed the inkling of suspicion that threatened to rear its cautious little head. He was the white doctor who would do what he thought best, and I was the inexperienced young girl who had to believe and trust in the process. Yet, I left his office with a niggling, underlying sense that I had been violated in some way, without having the terms of reference to structure these thoughts or articulate them. These thoughts lurked in the depths of my consciousness where they lay dormant for re-emergence when the time was ripe.

A few years later, allured by the call of all that was subversive, I dabbled with witchcraft and feminism. The witchcraft was not really for me. It was only remotely interesting when I thought it was about drinking your period blood, casting spells to draw nice stuff into your life and running around naked under a full moon. In addition, the drinking period blood bit was losing me friends. But the feminism ... Oh, the feminism ... The feminism kick-started a deep introspection, one where I retracted to a place deep within my core to engage with everything that I thought I knew. I went on a fantastical journey inside myself to discover who I was, what my values were and who I wanted to be. And confronted some deep-seated trauma in the process.

My journey into feminism was not only an intellectual one; it was quasi-spiritual in nature too. I catapulted myself outwards to look at the world around me, my surrounding contextual environment, and asked difficult questions about how we as people, as communities and societies, forge relationships; how we engage with each other and how the notion of power comes into play in all of this. I realised, with a sense of shock, that I had never claimed agency. I had never felt entitled to. My background and the socio-political context within which I had been raised in *apartheid* South Africa geared me towards being respectful, silent and a follower. It was both frightening and liberating to discover that my views mattered, that they need not conform and that I had a responsibility for staking claim, for speaking out and taking up space in the world – very different from my attempts to shy away, hide and silence my voice. I could diverge from the orthodox pathway and create new routes of my own. I need not follow, but instead, could dare to think about leading the way.

This was a period of the lights dawning for me. Suddenly, I was re-conceptualising my experiences through the prism of a gendered social order, with gendered interactions and power dynamics at play that determined how I was able to fit into the world and claim space in it. Even more mind-blowing, was the fact that these gendered interactions were taking place not just at an individual level, but at a societal level. They impacted on every social and public institution that I engaged with – my family, church, community, relationships, university, the state itself... the list was endless. And even more illuminating was the intersection between my gender, sexuality and other social variables such as being black in a country where apartheid was being dismantled, being a young person at the dawn of democracy and living in my demarcated community as designated by the Group Areas Act. All these aspects of identity criss-crossed in very significant ways. And finally, I was able to view the interactions with my childhood doctor and the gynaecologist through the lens of sexual violence, and its underlying power dynamics of established, affluent white men of the patriarchy doing what they did simply because they could.

It has been almost 30 years since I began my journey as a feminist. And here we are, at a juncture where arguably the most powerful nation in the world has elected to its highest office, a man who endorses pussy grabbing as a legitimate means of exercising control over women. President Trump was in office for a heartbeat, barely time to warm up his chair, and he had already shown signs of how his administration would affect the lives of women all over the world. The politics of accentuating differences and a sense of "otherness" amongst people is a normalised aspect of his leadership. The ban on the entry of certain Muslim nationals to the USA stands out as the single biggest overt act of discrimination, fuelling outcry amongst all of us who worry about living in a world that is not appreciative and tolerant of racial and cultural diversity. The political rhetoric of building walls and refusing entry into the USA is an important feature of President Trump's foreign relations agenda. It has fueled a problematic narrative that America can isolate itself and thrive as a self-sufficient nation state that is amputated from the rest of the world. It has encouraged and slapped prejudice on the back, and created an environment where closet fascists can creep out of the woodwork and preach their gospel of a perceived shared sense of identity in ways that incite tension and conflict.

We have come to expect the worst of the Trump administration, and rightfully so. With a sense of anxious inevitably, we know that he is bad news for human rights and social justice from all perspectives and intersections – nationality, race, class, gender and sexual orientation. We have resigned ourselves to waiting with bated breath and watching the horror of this drama play itself out. We worry that we are in some sort of bizarre time warp where, against our will, we have been catapulted backwards into a quasi-Neanderthal world, fuelled by a president who ranks women's looks and bodies in a 10-point system and sexualises his daughter and muses about dating her. It is indeed terrifying to realise this is a dream from which we are not waking, one that goes on in a wave of astonishing new onslaughts each day.

We know that President Trump is not alone in espousing sexist values; many men and women subscribe to them, but as a high profile public figure, he becomes the mouthpiece of an entrenched ideological stance of misogyny. We know that we have our own local leaders who espouse similar values. Yet, President Trump has the platform upon which to amplify these views on a world stage in ways that easily germinate and grow. Of particular concern is the opportunity for translating toxicity into public policy. We saw this with the reinstatement of the global "gag rule," otherwise known as the Mexico City Policy. The gag rule was instated by the Reagan administration in 1984, and sought to block federal international funding to non-governmental organisations that provided any sort of abortion counselling or service, even if these services are not directly funded by the USA.

The rule had a widespread impact on the lives and health of women and girls, particularly in the Global South. It negatively affected a wide range of critical services provided to women, such as those that address gender-based violence. The first few weeks of the Trump administration reinforced the reality that men will take life-altering decisions about women's sexual and reproductive rights without any pretence to hold public consultations. The Trump administration has the potential to significantly affect the global political agenda. It has, for example, become clear that President Trump has a negative view of the role of Africa on the global stage. His musings on "Nambia" and his views on African states as being "shithole" countries are indicative of stereotypical, racist views of the continent, which are likely to impact on policy stances. By 2018, President Trump still had not bothered to fill the vacant African Affairs senior leadership positions in the State Department, and there is no zeal to fill the position of Assistant Secretary for African Affairs and key ambassadorships on the continent, such as to South Africa, Somalia and Tanzania. With this lack of policy priority accorded to Africa, we have seen and will continue to see a negative impact on foreign aid allocated to the continent.

And yet … President Trump's first week in office also gave me tremendous hope. In the face of deep-seated fears that the administration was working fast to institutionalise values of white supremacy and misogyny, women across the globe decided, "Hell no, not under our watch!" And what followed is the stuff that miracles are made of. With a mission of challenging institutionalised patriarchy, hundreds of thousands of women took to streets in a surge of unprecedented social mobilisation. Cities around the world were alight with women fighting back and speaking out. A sea of clever, visceral posters attested to this dormant rage ignited by views that "pussies are for grabbing" and "women are young and beautiful pieces of ass." Little pink pussy ears bobbed around worldwide, signifiers not of "cuteness," but of defiance, agency and pushing back. And the message is abundantly clear – there is place for being Nasty Woman when we need to be. "Not as nasty as a swastika painted on a pride flag ... not as nasty as racism, fraud, conflict of interests, homophobia, sexual assault, transphobia, white supremacy, misogyny, ignorance, white privilege ..." but nasty as in "the battles my grandmothers fought to get me into that voting booth."[1] And while the marches were not without some serious shortcomings – they brought to the fore, for example, the fact that black women continue to be marginalised in social mobilisation campaigns, yet they still marked an important milestone in building international activism.

If the past few months have taught us anything, it is that we will not take misogyny lying down. As women, in our intersectionalism, we have agency and we will continue to find ways of claiming this and taking a stand – all in the name of making the world a more peaceful, tolerant and non-nasty place for everyone. To bring about social change, we need to be radical, we need to be angry, we need threats. We need revolutionary thought and action. Significant social transformation such as the right to vote, the right to choose abortion, the right to engage in same-sex relationships, are all aspects of social change that came about as a result of radical thought and action. Contemporary popular feminism's approach of sticking as closely as possible to the status quo is not bringing about fundamental change. The drive to sell feminism and render it universally acceptable, has resulted in a disavowal of the radical ideas that underpin it. At the end of the day, we have to ask ourselves, what has this really achieved? Donald Trump was still elected to power notwithstanding the popularisation of feminism.

Sandra Bartky[2] describes the process of becoming feminist as a profound personal transformation involving both changes in behaviour and in consciousness. The process of becoming feminist is not an end state, but an ongoing journey. It entails the development of a multiplicity of feminist consciousness, derived from involvement and interpretation of different situated experiences.

And here's the thing about feminism – in the personal journey of undergoing this profound personal transformation, we have to look beyond ourselves and take stock of the bigger picture, which necessarily entails a focus on the structural and systemic issues that affect women as a community and a society. We must think about the intersections between race, class, gender and sexual orientation in relation to power and privilege. And while there is nothing wrong with building a feminism that is empathetic and inclusive, it must be radical and push the envelope if we are serious about real change. Let the spirit of the global Women's Marches galvanise us.

Joy Watson is a senior researcher and feminist writer, with many years' experience in analysing public policy and legislation from a feminist perspective. Her work focuses on women and service delivery, women and governance, and violence against women, and she has been involved in both local and international research projects. She is integrally involved in feminist advocacy and has published widely as a policy brief specialist as well as in popular media. Joy has served on the boards of feminist organisations, and is currently the Chair of the Board of the Women on Farms Project. She is currently undertaking a PhD on rape and public policy formulation at the University of Stellenbosch and is the online editor for www.nastywomen.org.za.

MY ARMS ARE TIRED OF HOLDING THIS SIGN

Amanda Gouws

I have been holding this sign since the 1980s, when I became a feminist activist, while studying in the USA for my PhD in Political Science and Gender Studies. There are many slogans on my sign – "women's liberation," "the personal is political," "pro-choice," "I have the right to control my own body," "stop gender-based violence," "women are not door mats," "we need a child care facility,""women's rights are human rights," "we need sanitary pads," "biology is not destiny," "our feminism will be intersectional or it will be bullshit"...

The list goes on and my arms are tired. And yet, here I am. Thirty years later, we women are still holding up the same signs. With gravity pulling down our arms and our breasts, the past speaking to the present, while the present renders itself as crude, boorish, misogynist, dishonest, lying and populist presidents, both in the USA and in South Africa, under former President Zuma, and elsewhere. It did not escape us that Donald Trump's first executive order seriously eroded women's reproductive rights. An executive order signed by a man who thinks that pussies are only there to be grabbed, while we, the women, give birth, through that same vaginal channel, we bleed, we are violated through that very same vagina. What better display of male political power is there than to limit and deny women reproductive rights? It goes right to the heart of difference, to the heart of control over our bodies and our lives, to the heart of our desire, our pleasure, and our autonomy.

In South Africa, the ugly display of sexual violence reared up on its hind legs in the third week of May 2017, while I was writing this essay, as it does most weeks. Beautiful Karabo Mokoena was killed by her intimate partner, her body burnt beyond recognition, just because she wanted out of an abusive relationship. The week before that, four girls under the age of six disappeared and one was found raped and killed. We can recite incidents *ad nauseum*. The violations are, again, on the front pages of South African newspapers, as they always are when the stories are gruesome enough. Anene Booysen, raped and disembowled. Reeva Steenkamp, shot and killed by feted paralymphic athlete, Oscar Pistorius. They all become mere statistics. Women's outrage about sexual violence with impunity continues unabated, while the government goes about business as usual.

But it is not only the politics of spectacle on the front pages of our newspapers or in the chambers of the legislatures that make our arms tired, it is also what Rob Nixon conceptualises as "slow violence." He uses this concept to describe and analyse the environmental degradation that affects us all, but the poor most significantly.[3] "Slow violence" can also be applied to the erosion of gains that women have made over the past two to three decades and the depoliticisation of feminist activism, due to the invisible processes of neo-liberal globalisation and neo-liberal capitalism's consumer culture.

In a digital era of soundbite solutions, women are made to believe that they can achieve everything if only they concentrate on cultivating an image, buy the "right" clothes, the "right" make-up, the "right" underwear, and subscribe to a new age dietary regime to improve appearance and reduce weight. It makes us believe that women can be everything a man can be, we can be sexy and even predatory in our sexual behaviour. We only need to "lean in." This is the type of "equality" that focuses entirely on the individual, and on individualised solutions for collective social problems. It makes invisible the very real global systemic inequalities and oppressions that neo-liberal capital creates for all people and denies the feminisation of poverty globally.

George Monbiot wrote in *The Guardian* about neo-liberalism:

> ... the result is first disempowerment then disenfranchisement. If the dominant ideology stops governments from changing social outcomes, they can no longer respond to the needs of the electorate. Politics become irrelevant to people's lives; debate is reduced to the jabber of a remote elite. The disenfranchised turn instead to a virulent anti-politics in which facts and arguments are replaced by slogans, symbols and sensation.[4]

Globally, we now see anti-politics when political leaders are asked to account for their misreading of voters' needs, of which at least 50 percent are women. The populist politics *a la* Trump and Zuma have made it acceptable to lie or fabricate facts. Fake news. It is the slow violence of the neglect of women's needs. It is the slow violence of the denial of our common humanity. It is the slow violence of the erasure of our voices, that brings us back to the streets.

It was the Women's March the day after Trump was inaugurated that put feminist activism visibly back on the political agenda in the USA, and globally. It was the millions of pink "pussy" hats showing that women will not stand by to be grabbed and groped and silenced. The pussies and our male allies were out in the streets to show our collective power. In South Africa, it was young women students, calling themselves radical intersectional African feminists, that took to the streets topless in 2016, to end rape culture and reinvigorate feminist activism here. Protests spread around the country and forced universities to look into the traditions, practices and perceptions that normalise sexual violence. It was their visible angry presence, carrying sjamboks[5] that shouted "enough is enough!".

For the sake of a new generation of women, for the sake of our daughters (the daughters of the witches that were not burnt – as another poster declared), we cannot give up the struggle against women's oppression now or ever. We must expose unaccountable leadership, expose the limits of the quota system that put unaccountable women in legislatures, expose the limits of gender mainstreaming that gives us technocratic governance and the problem that if everyone has to take responsibility for gender, then nobody will. We must expose the pussy grabbing by men who boast about sexual violence.

We cannot let go of the signs now.

How long will we have to hold up these signs? As long as it takes!

Amanda Gouws is Professor of Political Science at the University of Stellenbosch, South Africa. She holds a South African Research Chair Inititative (SARChI) Chair in Gender Politics, and has published widely on women and citizenship, the National Gender Machinery, and women's representation. She is the editor of *(Un)Thinking Citizenship: Feminist Debates in Contemporary South Africa* (UK: Ashgate and Cape Town: Juta, 2005). Her edited book with Daiva Stasiulis as co-editor, *Gender and Multiculturalism: North/ South Perspectives* was published by Routledge Press in 2014 and UKZN Press, 2016. Amanda was a Commissioner for the South African Commission on Gender Equality from 2012–2014, and is a political commentator/writer for newspaper, radio and television. She is a feminist activist.

NASTY WOMEN RUN THE WORLD – RUNNING FOR AND FROM PUBLIC OFFICE

Raenette Gottardo

"I want you to know that nothing has made me prouder than to be your champion, and to all the little girls who are watching this, never doubt that you are valuable and powerful and deserving of every chance and opportunity in the world to pursue and achieve your own dreams."[6]

I have the most significant reverence and admiration for Hillary Rodham Clinton. I know she can be a polarising figure to many women, but her sheer tenacity and perseverance in public office over many decades resulted in my strong support for her candidacy for the Presidency of the United States of America, in both the 2008 and 2016 races.

I had such high expectations that she would succeed in the end. Following an, at times, brutal and bruising Presidential campaign where she shone brightly in all the Presidential debates – I had such high expectations that she would shatter the final glass ceiling of all.

It was not meant to be in 2008. And it was not meant to be in 2016. With the glass ceiling firmly intact in the highest office in the USA, I spent much of the campaign's aftermath in a state of mourning and deep and profound introspection about gender and public representation, mindful of my own experiences in South Africa's liberal constitutional order. These are experiences riddled with patriarchal power.

As hundreds of thousands of women took to the streets to march and protest in the aftermath of the election of Donald Trump, I found myself trapped in a torrent of unresolved emotion and an intellectual search for answers.

In my own case, it has been a complex stop-and-start career, which has spanned elected office, civil society leadership, academia and constitutional office at very tender ages, and asking difficult questions about the interplay of power relations, patriarchy and gender.

This very interplay made me both run for, and from, public office at various intervals. I profoundly identify with every woman who has ever run and served, or who is contemplating running, for office. I am pleased that more women are doing so in ever-growing numbers – and that there is a post-Trump bump in these statistics.

I personally wanted to run for office to confront this interplay of power and patriarchy, and I have equally run away from office, more than once, to escape the grubby claws of institutionalised patriarchal power that seeks to shape and mould the destiny of women.

As the youngest woman Member of Parliament in South Africa at the age of 27 in 1999 – a title I happily and gracefully handed to younger and newer generations of female representatives over time – and as my country's youngest Electoral Commissioner at the age of 39 in 2011, I have had ample experience and exposure to the deeper layer of dynamics that renders public life in South Africa a hostile space for women – especially intellectually qualified and accomplished women.

While there may be a significant number of women in public office in South Africa today – a magnificent achievement that is rightly hailed globally – the reality of party discipline and party hierarchy in the current system remains a patriarchal "boys club." While South Africa has its own discourse about the possibility of a woman President with her own set of professional achievements, the country still has this discourse in the shade of patriarchy.

Ironically, it was during my stint in Constitutional office that I learnt first-hand of the fallacies of gender unity and its dangers. A staggeringly sobering experience, a woman colleague had appealed to my sense of gender unity in order to dilute my focus on the law and on principle. When I resigned from the Independent Electoral Commission (IEC) for a host of complex reasons that are becoming clearer as time progresses in our body politic, I did so mindful of the space I was surrendering as a woman in a country with a majority female population that remains underrepresented in many spheres of public life.

Section 193(2) of the *Constitution of the Republic of South Africa*, Act 108 of 1996, requires that all Chapter Nine Constitutional institutions must "reflect broadly the race and gender composition of South Africa," which is a factor that "must be considered when members are appointed." When I look at the current ratio of male to female Commissioners at the IEC (4:1),[7] I often wonder whether this constitutional stipulation has been compromised. While I am co-responsible for this set of facts in the sense that I resigned from the IEC, it is lamentable and regrettable, and I remain filled with anguish for that loss.

As more women prepare to run for public office, I have had ample time to reflect on why I ran from it. I have come to accept that the only solution is to tilt the balance of the numbers, create environments that expose biases more clearly, and seek to 'de-bias environments' along the lines of behavioural economist and feminist scholar Professor Iris Bohnet's ground-breaking work from Harvard's Kennedy School Women in Public Policy Programme.[8]

Along this journey of private reflection and public roles there have been moments, like the Hillary ceiling-moment, that have stood out. The towering figure of German Chancellor Angela Merkel who has experienced her fair share of sexist moments, former Australian Prime Minister Julia Gillard's riveting and spine-chilling "misogyny" speech confronting Tony Abbott in 2010, Christine Lagarde's appointment as the International Monetary Fund's first woman Managing Director in 2011 (after the inglorious fall of Dominique Strauss Kahn), and Janet Yellen's nomination as first woman Chair of the Federal Reserve in 2014. Let these two dates sink in for a moment – the first women to ever fill these high finance, high power roles only took their places in 2011 and 2014!

I am equally encouraged that many of Europe's current Defence Ministers are women and that the activities of Emily's list in the USA and other Political Action Committees, both Republican and Democrat, focus on securing more women into Congress and the Senate, respectively.

What bothers me significantly though, is that while South Africa has a watered-down version of the debate to elect a woman President as part of a political party's succession struggles, we are not asking about the decline in women representation in public life in South Africa and the Southern African Development Community (SADC) region more broadly. Gender Links, a Gauteng-based organisation, points out that we should all be profoundly alarmed and engaged with the decline in women's representation in political decision-making, following the 2014 national and provincial elections.

Moreover, South Africa has seen a noticeable and disconcerting increase in the number of male-only panels in areas as diverse as economic policy, policy and political analysis, and constitutional law, at conferences and symposia over the past ten years.

Column spaces and opinion pieces written by women on policy matters have diminished dramatically and the numbers of women in public office, while relatively high by global standards, have diminished rather sadly.

What I have learnt from my research in this area, from my various experiences, and from all of this, is that I am not a stereotype. I am a norm of sorts, in a constructivist sense. A norm in a world where Nasty Women do not run the world – at least not yet.

What I am encouraged by, is that my deep desire to run for office and address the injustice of gender disparity has inevitably led to a public path, and I am partly comforted by the fact that my decision to run from the more egregious aspects of patriarchal power is not atypical.[9]

What this has taught me at a profound level, though, as a sort of "forever-activist," is the deep and profound need to not only ensure that many Nasty Women run for office, but that we form such a formidable substructure, subculture and sub-strata of support for one another when we get there, that nothing and no exercise of crude patriarchal power will force us to run from it ever again.[10]

I have decided, upon reflection, that I would indeed do it all over again – but differently. I would never run from it again knowing now what I ought to have prepared for then: I would be ever more confrontational about patriarchal power until Nasty Women do run the world! And I would run with the pack of she-wolves who make that happen.[11]

Raenette Gottardo holds a BA (Law), Hons (IR) cum laude and an MA (International Relations) cum laude from the University of Johannesburg and an MSc (Public Policy and Administration) cum laude from the London School of Economics. In 1999, she became the youngest woman elected to the South African parliament under its new Constitutional order. Raenette became a Yale Greenberg Fellow in 2003, and is a Young Global Leader of the World Economic Forum, Fellow of the Emerging Leaders Programme of the Centre for Leadership and Public Values at Duke University and the University of Cape Town, and an ALI Aspen Institute Fellow. Raenette has served her country as a member of the Electoral Commission of the Republic of South Africa, and has taught and guest lectured extensively. She now consults in Public policy, International Relations and gender. Raenette's book *Up in Arms: The Search for Accountability for the Arms Deal in Parliament* was published by Jacana (2012).

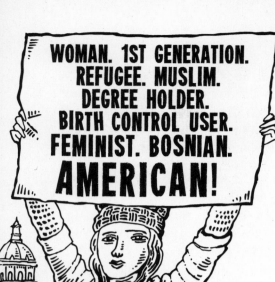

WOMAN. 1ST GENERATION.
REFUGEE. MUSLIM.
DEGREE HOLDER.
BIRTH CONTROL USER.
FEMINIST. BOSNIAN.
AMERICAN!

LESSONS ABOUT RESILIENCE, STRUGGLE, RESISTANCE AND DETERMINATION

Nidžara Ahmetašević

In September 2016, I met four sisters from Kabul in the park near the train station in Thessaloniki, Greece. They were amongst hundreds of people living on the streets while trying to cross the border toward Macedonia, to continue their journey toward what they believe is freedom and peace – the Global North. Together with their brother, they were on the road for over a year.

We gelled immediately. I spotted the sisters in one corner of the park where they had been sleeping for over three weeks. They were trying to cross the closed border, with no success, and would usually leave at around sunset and walk toward the Macedonian border. Sometimes they managed to take a train and stay on in the city nearest to the border, and would then go out and try to cross. Again and again.

When we met, they were so tired that they could not stand. The night before, they had again tried to cross. Exhausted, the women invited me to sit down on the thin mat they shared. They could not sleep in the middle of the day in a park full of people. They could not find rest, or a break. Their food was donated by volunteers. They used bathrooms and toilets in nearby train stations, afraid someone would prevent them from entering, which happened from time to time.

Each of the five of them had a small backpack, thin mats and nothing else. I accepted their invitation to sit down, and from that moment on, I had a new family. They wanted to talk about something other than the ugly reality of their everyday life. And I could understand that need. More than 20 years before I had met the sisters, I too was a refugee, running from the war in Sarajevo. Most of the time I had just needed a friend, somebody to talk to about normal life. I did not want to be pitied or looked at as a case to feel sorry for. The sisters wanted to talk about literature and fashion. Two had studied comparative literature as had I, and one was into fashion. We laughed and talked about books, dresses and colours that we like. We did not mention their trip from the previous night; we did not talk about the park and life on the streets. We did not talk about their perilous journey that seemed to go on forever.

For the remainder of our days in Thessaloniki, we tried to stay close to each other. We talked about everything, we tried to laugh together, and we were sad together. I tried to encourage them to continue their journey and to be brave. They promised me that we would meet again, far away from Thessaloniki.

They were so brave and went through such unimaginable trials to get to a country where they could feel safe. We are still in touch. I have visited them in their new home. They cooked for me. We talked for hours. I listened to their stories about resistance and feminism under conditions that were so hard for me to understand. War, fear, uncertainty, poverty and constant struggle. I cannot number all the life lessons I learnt from them. We exchanged a lot, too. I have lived through war, siege, and was a refugee for some time. I know what it's like to live with fear and to live in a crazy post-conflict country where every day is an endeavour, and where this goes on for decades. Incomparable to their life, but somehow, we understood each other.

What strikes me the most about each of the sisters is their constant and strong thrust to learn something new. Their eyes are wide open, as are their hearts.

In 2017, in April, I went to Sid, a small town in Serbia at the border of Croatia. Nearby is an even smaller town, Adasevci. I drove toward Adasevci on the highway. At one point, on the side, I saw an old socialist-style motel and a nearby modern gas station. The motel and surrounding area have been converted into a refugee camp that looks apocalyptic. The whole scenario was surreal.

From the highway, I enter a parking area in front of the gas station, which is nice and clean, with air conditioning and people on a coffee break. At the back, however, are broken fences, big tents, guards, lots of children running around, and lonely lost people sitting around and trying to find ways to pass their days. At one corner, I spot three women. They are laughing from their hearts. Laughing like they are in the middle of the coolest bar in New York City, having the time of their life.

Happily, they accept me in their small circle and tell me their stories. They are in their thirties, from Syria. They started their journey six months before. Somewhere along the way, a smuggler robbed them of their money and documents, and they are stuck in Serbia in the camp of nightmares. Their families are in Germany, but they cannot find a way to get there legally. The borders are closed. They laugh about both their dreams and their reality. They invite me to the camp with them. In order to enter, I need permission from the Government of Serbia. The women tell me, "It is okay. You are with us."

We enter through a broken fence. They take me to their tent, at the very end of a long row of big, ugly tents. I peek inside. Military cots, fitted tightly next to each other; floors covered with ugly gray military blankets. It looks like a concentration camp from the early 1990s in Bosnia. The women share this tent with over 100 people. I enter their space. Cots covered with gray blankets that function as sheets, pillows and walls, all at the same time. There is nothing inside. Nothing. Just a couple of personal things the women keep with them. There is no space for anything else. Under one bed is a big black bag, and inside is coffee and a small gas cooker. "Let's go to the jungle. We invite you for coffee."

And I follow. By the camp, there is a small grove. We enter through the bushes, and it's like we have entered a parallel world. People are on the ground everywhere. Some are just sitting and doing nothing. Some are playing on their phones. Some are spending time with their families while drinking tea or coffee. "This is where we come to have some quiet time. In the camp, it is not possible. Not even at night. We all come here. We make a fire and cook here too. The food in the camp is not good, so we buy food in the city and cook it here. But most of the time we just come to be in peace," the women tell me. We find a spot, they make the coffee and serve it in plastic cups. We sit in the peace of woods around us and chat. One of the women was an English Professor at the University in Damascus. Another is a lawyer. The third is an IT expert. After a while, I leave. They stay on in the jungle to cook lunch.

These are just some of the stories I have encountered over the past two-and-a-half years on a refugee route in the Balkans. All of the stories are lessons about resilience, struggle, resistance and determination. But they are also stories about people whose hearts are wide open, despite the traumatic experiences they have gone through and are still going through. Instead of welcoming them, the Global North decided to close its borders and build not only physical walls, but to encourage walls of prejudice that are much harder to cross, dismantle or destroy.

Talking about refugees and migrants, engaging and being active in promoting their rights and spreading their stories is crucial for feminism today. This is what solidarity means today. As feminists, we have to act, while at the same time be open to learning from voices of resilience and courage, told by women and men who are embarking on this perilous journey. What they bring to us is new cultures, new ideas, new approaches to different things, things that will make us better people. We have to give them something in return, and together we can then find a way to break down any wall.

Nidžara Ahmetašević has a long career as a journalist working for local, regional and international media on human rights, war crimes, international affairs and migration. Her work has been published in *The New Yorker*, *Al Jazeera English* online, *The Observer*, *The Guardian*, *The Independent on Sunday*, the *International Justice Tribune*, *Balkan Insight* and *EU Observer*, amongst others. Nidžara has been awarded in Bosnia and internationally, including the AHDA Columbia University Fellowship, Chevening Scholarship, Ron Brown Fellowship for Young Professionals, and UNICEF Keizo Obuchi Award.

DON'T FORGET: WHITE WOMEN VOTED FOR TRUMP

Ashanti Kunene

In the unprecedented 2016 US election, businessman turned television personality Donald J. Trump was elected as the 45th President of the United States of America (POTUS) and assumed office on 20 January 2017. Trump beat seasoned politician Hillary Rodham Clinton, who, had she won, would have been the first woman president of the country. Over and above the shock of Trump becoming POTUS, was the fact that it was white women that helped get him into office, despite his well-documented history of sexism and misogyny.[12] Trump won 53 percent of white women's votes, and in the three states that decided the election – Wisconsin, Pennsylvania and Michigan – this margin was enough to send him to the White House.[13]

In an article penned for the *Atlantic*, author Ta-Nehisi Coates explains how the election of Donald Trump was in essence the preservation of white supremacy, for his presidency is founded on the negation of Barack Obama's legacy as America's first African American president.[14] Arguably, white women have historically helped their white husbands uphold white supremacy,[15] choosing their relative comfort and ability to shape their own futures over the safety of black and brown people, and all people of colour (POCs).

Christine Hutchison, a San Francisco-based PhD psychology student with the Wright Institute, argues[16] that this 53 percent of white women who cast their vote for Trump in 2016, did so out of both internalised oppression and dominance. She argues:

> White women have experienced the oppression and violence done to our gender as well as the privilege and dominance we have been handed in accordance with our race, and so our unconscious holds the sexism done against us and [it also holds] the racism done by us. We are not consciously racist, but we benefit from continued white supremacy by uncritically accepting our relative safety and our ability to shape our own future. We decide to believe racism is the occasional one-off act of violence, which we decry, not acknowledging that our daily decisions of where to live, what to buy and whose voices we share with our white communities are all ways we participate in racism. We believe, unconsciously, that our own comfort is more important than the safety of people of color.

The United States Suffrage movement, which secured white women's right to vote on 18 August 1920, is an early example of the historical maligning of black women by largely white feminist movements that fail to address the gendered and racial subjugation of black women. It would take another 45 years for the Voting Rights Act of 1965 to pass, securing black women's right to vote.[17] The sentiment that white women activists work largely for the preservation of white supremacy rather than equal rights is a historical lament that one can trace all the way back to Sojourner Truth and her famous 1851 "Ain't I a Woman?" speech.

In an opinion piece[18] penned for *Color Lines*, Jamilah Lemieux lists all the reasons why she, as a black woman, afforded herself "the emotional frailty usually reserved for white women" and did not attend the Women's March on 21 January 2017. She maintains that, "It won't serve my own mental health needs to put my body on the line to feign solidarity with women who by and large did not have my back prior to November". Lemieux is one of the black women that did not attend – because black women consistently show up for humanity even though humanity does not show up for us. Many black women did attend the Women's March, if anything, to hold white women accountable and remind them that white women did indeed put Trump in power.

Bob Bland, a fashion designer who was part of the March's brainstorming process wrote in a public statement that "the reality is that the women who initially started organising the march were almost all white."[19] In response to the backlash about the Women's March being perceived as a white woman's march, Heidi Solomon-Orlick (one of the co-organisers of the Pennsylvania chapter of the Women's March, in an interview with *Teen Vogue*) said, "We needed to quickly mobilise ... to add diversity."

That diversity is treated like an after-thought; added after the fact, it is precisely why black women felt the Women's March was disingenuous. Intersectionality is much more than the idea that we must "add black womxn, POCs, queers, and stir." That the March was conceivably organised to the exclusion of black women, only brought on board to add a sprinkle of colour, is one of the reasons why black women feel the Women's March was exclusive, rather than inclusive, of all womxn. Thousands of white women showed up for the Women's March, but are nowhere to be found when it comes to the Black Lives Matter movement.

The narrative of the Women's March is portrayed as positive and inspiring, whereas the *Black Lives Matter* protests are seen as socially divisive – and on the racially-biased spectrum of violence, black people protesting for equal rights are at least, inconvenient and at worst, an all-out rebellion in need of violent repression. In her *Color Lines* article, *Black Lives* Matter Organiser Miski Noor[20] explains how white lives matter more than black lives:

> [The] system works exactly as it is intended to: to protect Whiteness in general and White womanhood in particular. The long history of the state protecting the supposed sanctity of White womanhood[21] is one of the primary functions of US institutions, systems and culture. From the violence visited

upon Black youth in the name of White womanhood, as in the case of Emmett Till,[22] or in the use of Black women's bodies for surreptitious and dangerous medical experimentation, like in the case of Henrietta Lacks,[23] White women are protected at the expense of the lives of Black people.

And it is precisely this double standard that the "Don't Forget, White Women Voted for Trump" poster speaks to. So, while the Women's March was a show of solidarity, it is important to remember that just because there is a women's movement does not mean that the movement is necessarily feminist; or that the brand of feminism eschewed is intersectional. Intersectionality as praxis is one of the key issues that came up in criticism of the Women's March. And it is because of intersectionality that Trump's election as POTUS offers a very unique opportunity.

The opportunity Trump offers is a call to engage in serious conversation about how we as the human family have structured our lives, how power is used to render people voiceless and lifeless, how we engage and live with one another as members of a society, and how our actions thus far have degraded the planet. As so-called feminists, whether liberal, radical, black militant or mostly white and mainstream, we need to reflect on our praxis. We need a feminist praxis that is not selective about the injustices that we rage and march against. Trump's presence in the White House offers an everyday reminder that we have to be better than our parents and grandparents, and we have to try to do better. Trump's election forces us to have honest conversations (with each other) and practice intersectionality as the revolutionary praxis that it is – and not a white-washed intersectionality that is nothing more than a sophisticated version of identity politics.

Intersectionality is more than an analytical perspective. It is inherently about praxis. It does not help simply knowing your positionality, the important question is – do your everyday actions reflect this knowing? Did you march because you want to change the white supremacist, anti-black, anti-poor, capitalistic heteronormative system? Or, did you march because you had FOMO (fear of missing out) and wanted to wear a knitted pink pussy hat just like all the other Nasty Women? These are questions we must ask ourselves, conversations we must have soon, because at some point black womxn are going to stop showing up for humanity. It's enough. We are enough.

Ashanti Kunene is an International Studies Masters student, linked to the SARChI Chair in Gender Politics at the University of Stellenbosch. Passionate about social justice issues Ashanti seeks to upend the established knowledge power structures that perpetuate epistemic oppression. Her research interests include humans and how their collective epistemological and ontological inclinations shape and drive society. Ashanti was identified as a student leader during the 2015-2016 #FeesMustFall student movement at the University of Stellenbosch. Ashanti smashes patriarchy every day with her stiletto heels.

BUILD BRIDGES NOT WALLS

Daiva Stasiulis

Amongst the copious campaign promises in real estate magnate and reality television star Donald Trump's 2016 improbable bid for the White House, perhaps the most preposterous was his pledge that he would build an "impenetrable physical wall" along the southern border with Mexico – and that he would make Mexico pay for it. During the global march of women, timed to coincide with a worldwide protest against the United States presidential inauguration of Trump, banners reading "Build Bridges Not Walls" were dropped over numerous bridges and exterior walls. Clearly, many people in the USA rejected both this wall and what it represented in terms of exclusion and dehumanisation of migrants entering the country across its southern border.

In Trump's Manichean Twittersphere – where all nations, peoples and objects are either "nasty" or "tremendous," his imagined wall sat on the "beautiful" side of the ledger, while Mexican immigrants whom this wall was designed to keep out were grotesquely branded as criminals – rapists, murderers and drug dealers. Trump, boasting of his questionable credibility as a builder ("nobody builds walls better than me, believe me"), envisaged the "great wall" to be one foot taller than the Great Wall of China, "artistically beautiful," constructed of hardened concrete, rebar and steel. It would traverse about 1,000 miles (1,609 kilometres) of the nearly 2,000-mile border between the USA and Mexico, interrupted by natural barriers and, if needed, substitute fencing for concrete. To ensure its impenetrability, the wall was to be supplemented with "above and below ground sensors, towers, aerial surveillance," and at least 5,000 additional border patrol agents, significantly buttressing what is already a heavily fenced, patrolled and militarised border. Official estimates of building this wall have ranged from 22 to 67 billion USD, proclaimed by Trump to be paid for by Mexico in what can only be regarded as a complicated form of state extortion by the USA of its southern neighbour.[24]

To many people who have made the hazardous crossing into the USA in search of a better life, to secure work, reunite with their families, or escape violence in their troubled homelands (be it Central America, South America or further afield), the Trump border wall is already a reality. A frightening 700 of the frontier's 2,000 miles are already border-fenced, although none of this barrier could be described as either beautiful or impenetrable. The number of border patrol agents deployed along the United States southern boundary has increased five-fold since the early 1990s, under both the Clinton and George W. Bush administrations. In addition, a key strategy of the US "War on Drugs" was to funnel illicit border crossers toward areas deemed too treacherous to cross, such as Arizona's deserts, in the hopes that nature would take care of the "problem." Yet, far from deterring drug trafficking by wily drug cartels, the result since the year 2000, has been the deaths of an estimated 2,000 desperate migrants from heat, exhaustion and water deprivation.[25]

Many people who have successfully made it north of the border are amongst the legions of mostly "unauthorised" migrants that keep the country going – such as women household labourers, cleaning and caring for children and the elderly in American middle and upper class homes across the American South. Many others form an army of blue-collar workers toiling in jobs under conditions avoided by citizen-workers, forming 20-25 percent of the US national workforce in farming, fishing and forestry, domestic work, groundskeeping, clothing manufacture, construction and mining. In some states, these people perform a sizeable proportion of low-level service jobs in the hospitality sector. About two-thirds of this unauthorised workforce has resided in the USA for at least 10 years, their undocumented status and deportability rendering them especially vulnerable and exploitable. The ubiquity of undocumented workers from Mexico, elsewhere in Central and South America, and increasingly from Asia, is apparent in low skill, low wage jobs. Their prevalence in jobs with the harshest and/or most repulsive conditions such as crop picking, farming and animal slaughter has increased.

The appeal of Trump's wall to his predominantly white, less educated and ideologically conservative voters rests on the dubious claim that halting the entry of unauthorised migrants across the southern border would assist in "making America great again" by protecting American citizen-workers from competition and undercutting by undocumented workers.[26] This piece of sophistry ignores the blatant fact that people without legal status in the USA most often work in lower level jobs and suffer conditions spurned by those with status. The abysmally low wages and extreme hazardous and unprotected work conditions of temporary or undocumented migrants in the agri-business sectors are the reason that US supermarkets are crowded with plentiful and, for the middle class, affordable fresh produce. Scores of female caregivers and domestic workers from poor countries in Latin America and the larger global South, hidden in households, provide the care foundation for two-income families and assist wealthier women to more easily navigate the demands of their "double day." Having childcare and eldercare has thus become privately affordable for the more privileged classes – in a country that has ideologically defined universal social programmes as un-American.[27]

While there are aesthetically beautiful walls and fences – adorned with flowering vines or striking murals for instance, and walls that serve key environmental and social purposes such as shelter and weight-bearing, the types of walls built to divide nations and people are distinctly unbeautiful in a social sense. From the second century erection of Hadrian's Wall to separate Romans from the "barbarians," to the Israeli West Bank "Separation Barrier," walls have been constructed by rulers to dispossess, enclose, defend and keep out, based on differences in social wealth, nationality, ethnicity, race, gender and legal-juridical status. Historically, walls have marked imperial strategies to contain, segregate and displace indigenous peoples from their traditional territories, nascent capitalism (as in the late 18th century English enclosure movement), and stark ideological distinctions. They have reinforced fear of the "Other," emptying the citizenry of their humanity by concretely walling off those who are the epitome of Agamben's *homines sacri* (capable of being killed by anyone but not murdered or sacrificed by the state). Collectively constituted as a threat to something equally abstract as the "sovereignty of the nation state," today's autonomous migrants and asylum seekers only become momentarily humanised if they are aestheticised to seem heart-achingly innocent and lovely (witness the sympathetic response to the iconic 2015 photograph of three-year-old Aylan Kurdi tragically washed up on the shores of the Mediterranean).

At the extreme, walls represent the unmarked deaths of the desperate, the dehumanised Others who attempt to scale over or burrow under such walls rendered impassable by surveillance, electrocution and automatic weaponry. Many modern walls are built to demarcate and defend on behalf of and against nations, peoples and even 'civilisations.' Until recently, the Berlin Wall separating West from East Germany was viewed as the most horrific post-World War Two 'Cold War' barrier, resulting in the killing and deaths of at least 139 people, a number that today, pales in comparison to the several thousands who have died in recent years seeking sanctuary in increasingly walled-off European countries.

In Europe, tightening of border controls has been supplemented by the copious construction of walls to keep out unwanted migrants and refugees who are fleeing famine, environmental disaster and conflict. In 2012, Greece built a fence and electronic surveillance system along its border with Turkey to stem the sharp rise in undocumented migrants. Since 2015, Bulgaria, Hungary, Slovenia, Macedonia, Austria, and France have all erected walls or barbed wire-topped fences to halt the tide of poor and conflict-weary migrants flowing into these relatively wealthier countries. While many of these walls separate European Union (EU) nations from states outside the continental bloc, others are between EU states, including members of Europe's passport-free zone – reflecting how exclusion of what euphemistically were called "third country nationals" is one of the few common goals left of the tattered European Union. Such walls serve to divert, rather than halt, migrants who turn to people-smugglers and other dangerous routes to enter more northern countries. The result has been carnage. An unprecedented number of migrant deaths (more than 5,000 recorded in 2016 alone) have occurred during attempted crossings in overloaded boats on the Mediterranean Sea. To give Trump's most powerful 'Nasty Woman,' Angela Merkel, her due, the German Chancellor has distinguished herself in leading Germany's acceptance of more asylum-seekers than the rest of all EU countries combined. In a Europe dominated by wall-builders, holding a fragment of the Berlin Wall to symbolise the Cold War, Merkel addressed NATO leaders stating, "It is not isolation and the building of walls that make us successful, but open societies that are built on common values."[28]

The specific physical barrier invoked by Trump as a model for his wall was that erected by Israel, the system of fences and concrete walls constructed in 2002 following the second Palestinian "intifada" (uprising) along and inside the West Bank, to severely restrict the movement of Palestinians into Israel.[29] While Israeli officials refer to the barrier as an "anti-terror obstacle," Palestinians and social justice movements worldwide routinely refer to the Separation Wall as an "*apartheid* wall" signaling further aggressive efforts of the Israeli government to increase its territory in the ongoing occupation of Palestinians and the West Bank. This particular barrier exemplifies how walls simultaenously keep out and imprison people, to varying physical, legal and ideological degrees.

The USA is similarly all too familiar with ideological walls and legal barriers, from Jim Crow to the 13th Amendment, the "War on Drugs", the privatised prison system and present-day voting patterns. The second major "wall" in Trump's cynical and self-interested[30] migration policy was his executive order of a "Muslim ban," which imposed a total travel ban on people from Iran, Iraq, Somalia, Sudan, Yemen, Syria and Libya (with Iraq dropped from the list on Trump's second executive order). While the wall bordering Mexico constructs a physical obstacle to accessing US territory, the Muslim ban creates a legal-juridical barrier to entering the country. His first iteration of the Muslim travel ban was immediately met with extraordinary spontaneous protests of tens of thousands of people in over 80 airports across the United States, carrying signs of welcome and support to refugees and Muslims. Since then, the ban has repeatedly been challenged by federal judges, and temporarily halted on constitutional grounds involving violation of protections against religious discrimination. A hugely divisive issue, the ban, however, has the support (as reported in February 2017 surveys) of just over half of surveyed Americans. Despite judicial and popular challenge, Trump's executive orders have created chaos and increased Islamophobia at the borders and within the USA, and have massively disrupted the lives of Muslims and other people of colour living across the country.

Sadly, Trump is neither the first nor last cynical politician in the USA, or elsewhere, to win votes and build a populist base using the politics of fear and incitement of hatred. In Trump's landscape of numerous enemies within the United States, including the news media, judiciary, FBI, and strong-willed individuals who stand up and critique his erratic sexist, racist and homophobic policies and actions, his war against minorities within the USA trades heavily on anti-black stereotypes. This reality has not been lost amongst African-Americans, who have overwhelmingly opposed Trump and his unvarnished support for racialised law enforcement. His rise and this support has been linked to an unprecedented increase in police shootings and deaths of unarmed black people across the USA, as well as routine acquittals of the accused.[31]

In response to neighborhood vigilante George Zimmerman's acquittal in the 2012 Florida shooting of 17-year-old African American Trayvon Martin, *Black Lives Matter (BLM)* emerged as a ferocious movement across the United States (and major Canadian cities that have experienced similar patterns of shootings), protesting the routine use of lethal force against African Americans that rarely leads to conviction or incarceration of those wielding the guns. Many shootings of black people committed by police and citizens, such as in the case of Trayvon Martin, reveal an internal segregation and racialised bordering within the USA and Canada, where black teenagers are regarded as marauding intruders of violent intent within invisibly-gated socially homogenous, white neighbourhoods. The Black Lives Matter movement seeks to put "an end to the erasure of black lives and ... systems of racist power anchored in a history of white supremacy ... by seeking to influence city, state and federal policies through acts of protest and civil disobedience."[32] In some communities, Black Lives Matter has achieved progress, including equipping officers with body cameras that have recorded controversial and even fatal acts of policing in African American communities. Although the lethal uses of force against unarmed African Americans galvanising Black Lives Matter have unfortunately not abated, the movement has deepened and broadened its focus, strategies and alliances since Trump's November 2016 electoral victory. Building bridges between movements is frequently the Achilles Heel of social justice causes, whereby co-defining the enemy is easier than agreeing upon priorities, strategies and visions of a broad-based progressive movement.

In response to the perceived interrelatedness of Trump's attacks on Muslims, immigrants, asylum-seekers, women's reproductive rights, LGBTIQ rights, and the embattled labour movement, the priority of *Black Lives Matter* activists has shifted from protest to policy – to building bridges with other networked movements into a social justice coalition, inclusively self-titled as "The Majority."[33] This is a brilliant moniker for progressive movements that are routinely undermined through right-wing discourse as representing "special interests" that oppose the so-called and socially conservative "silent majority." As The Majority Movement matures, it is defining activism in terms of bridging the divide between street-level protests and electoral politics, between tearing down and building up, and between performing locally, and connecting globally. The movement, and social justice networks within it, are intent on building bridges and tearing down walls.

Daiva Stasiulis is Professor of Sociology at Carleton University (Ottawa, Canada). She is a feminist scholar working on intersectionality, and the nexus between citizenship and migration. The focus of her publications has been on the role played by immigration, and multiethnic and multi-racial diversity and inequalities in shaping the Canadian economy, politics and culture; and the opportunities and constraints of globalisation and settler colonisation in affecting migrants' lives and identities. Her book with Abigail Bakan, *Negotiating Citizenship: Migrant Women in Canada and the Global System* won the award for Best Book in Canadian Women's Studies in 2007. She edited a book with Amanda Gouws, *Gender and Multiculturalism: North-South Perspectives* (2014), and is currently completing a book entitled *The Emotional Cartography of Dual Citizenship: The Lebanese Diaspora in the Shadow of War* (for which she received the Marston Lafrance Research Award in 2016). Daiva's current anti-wall activism is focused on ending statelessness in Canada.

"I DID TRY AND FUCK HER.
SHE WAS MARRIED.
I MOVED ON HER LIKE A BITCH,
BUT I COULDN'T GET THERE.
AND SHE WAS MARRIED.
YOU KNOW I'M AUTOMATICALLY
ATTRACTED TO BEAUTIFUL.
I JUST START KISSING THEM.
IT'S LIKE A MAGNET.
JUST KISS.
I DON'T EVEN WAIT.
AND WHEN YOU'RE A STAR
THEY LET YOU DO IT.
YOU CAN DO ANYTHING...
GRAB THEM BY THE PUSSY.
YOU CAN DO ANYTHING."

THE PRESIDENT OF THE USA

HAUNTING

Kate True

"These words should haunt President Trump and embolden American women." - *Marilyn Minter*

On International Women's Day in March 2017, a poster appeared on walls all over New York City. Reminiscent of a memorial plaque found in front of a statue or in a building lobby, the image, in gold and bronze tones, features Trump's grinning face and what has been dubbed[34] his "sexual assault monologue;" the text of the infamous recording from Access Hollywood. The poster was created by the artist Marilyn Minter, as part of the Halt Action Group (HAG). HAG is an artist-activist coalition whose members also include curator Alison Gingeras and graffiti artist, KATSU. Although variations on this concept had been seen at the many Women's Marches in January 2017, this version, which quickly spread around the world via social media and a free downloadable PDF,[35] brilliantly sums up our current era. It is hideous and self-aggrandising at first glance, like Trump's penchant for the gold-plated branding of his name. But spend another moment looking, and you are pulled back to the sickening reality that the current United States president uttered these vile and violent words, and the effect is visceral, inciting us to anger and action.

I distinctly remember where I was the night that the Access Hollywood tape of Trump declaring, "I don't even wait. And when you're a star, they let you do it. You can do anything. Grab them by the pussy."[36] was first aired. I was in the middle of an Italian deli waiting for takeout. Glancing up to the wall at the blaring television as I waited for my late night tiramisu, it took just a few moments for the meaning of this story to sink in. I was sickened but not surprised; I lost my appetite.

As a resident of New York in the 1990s, during the aftermath of the Central Park jogger trial, I was disgusted by Donald Trump's racism and callous disregard for social justice, and the law. The *Central Park Five*, four of whom were black and one Hispanic, had been wrongfully accused and convicted of the beating and rape of a young white woman, Trisha Meili. Shortly after the arrests, Donald Trump – who was at the time a real estate mogul not involved in politics – took out an inflammatory full-page ad in the New York Times at an estimated cost of 85,000 USD, calling for a return of the death penalty. This was his first foray into public life.

Trump's incendiary advertisement played a role in securing a conviction for the innocent *Central Park Five*, according to one of the defendant's lawyers Michael Warren, who said that Trump "poisoned the minds of many people who lived in New York City and who, rightfully, had a natural affinity for the victim." Years later another man, already in prison on an unrelated rape charge, confessed to the Central Park jogger assault and rape, and DNA evidence corroborated it. All five young men (juveniles under the age of 18 at the time of conviction) served between six and 13 years each, before finally being released and fully exonerated.

During the election campaign, in October 2016, Trump doubled down on his claims about the *Central Park Five*, stating that he still thought they were guilty. This is after the men had been acquitted and won a 41 million USD suit against the city of New York. With this ludicrous and hateful statement, Trump showed his true colours once again, as a racist madman with no regard for science or actual fact, just for his own bigoted worldview. When the Access Hollywood tape came out days later, the uproar far outweighed that of Trump's *Central Park Five* comments. In my mind, the horror and dismay braided together, tightening into a knot on election day, and worsening ever since.

As an artist, I have faith in the power of images to inspire and incite, to educate and awaken. Marilyn Minter, with her brilliant image-creation, has placed Trump's nasty words front and centre, to embolden us all, lest we forget. Trump's words about the *Central Park Five* may have slipped from public memory, but I am hopeful that his sexual assault monologue will always stick to him. I would say haunt him, but this would only be possible if he had a conscience. However these words, and the work of Marilyn Minter and other artist-activists, will continue to haunt me, and to galvanise my resistance.

Kate True is a painter, portrait artist and curator in Boston, Massachusetts. She studied at Wesleyan University, where she received a Bachelors of Arts Degree with High Honours, and New York University where she received her Masters in Fine Arts Degree. Kate's prints and paintings have been featured in galleries around the United States of America, and are in thousands of private collections around the world. A Massachusetts Cultural Council grant recipient for the exhibit "Little Women," Kate has curated four shows in the past decade. She was the principal organiser behind Nasty Women Boston, a resistance art exhibit and fundraiser at Laconia Gallery Boston in September 2017. Kate also created the cover and part page artwork for this collection of feminist essays, *Nasty Women Talk Back*.

THE PERSONAL IS POLITICAL: FEMINIST NARRATIVES OF PERSONAL STORIES AS POLITICAL STORIES

WOMEN'S RIGHTS ARE HUMAN RIGHTS

Avni Amin

For someone whose job it is to promote gender equality and women's rights at a United Nations agency in Geneva, I can cite countless statistics showing how girls and women are discriminated against in virtually every part of the world. Like millions of women, waking up on 9 November 2016, I felt like I had been punched in the gut. I, too, had wanted to see history being made – not only the first woman, but a feminist president in the United States. I, too, had wanted to see one of the most qualified candidates with a record of public service and of defending the rights of the working class, children and women, become president. So I want to tell you about why I marched and my journey to becoming a feminist, growing up in India, a deeply misogynist society.

I am the eldest of two daughters. My father proudly claimed that daughters were all he ever wanted, challenging norms in a society that values only sons. We grew up in Mumbai on the western coast of India. We lived together with my father's brother's widow, my aunt, and her five children. For as long as I could remember, my aunt wore white saris – widows in Indian society were required to wear white clothes, no jewelry or make up, and were considered to bring bad luck. My aunt married at the age of 14. She was "persuaded" to marry her uncle and guardian who told her he would jump out of a window if she did not agree. By the age of 16, she had had her first child and by 26, she was a widow with five children – the youngest only two years old.

My aunt told me her story when I was a teenager. I remember feeling angry at how unfairly she had been treated. I recall thinking that if she had been able to complete her education, she would not have struggled financially after my uncle died. She, however, accepted that this was how it was. She had other dreams for me. Like my father, she hoped I would become a doctor or a scientist. My father taught my sister and me to dream big. We were sent to a private school and encouraged to excel.

Despite the security of knowing that I was valued in my family, Indian society has many ways to remind you of your "place" as a woman. A careless comment by an uncle about my dark skin and how it would not fetch me a good husband. A female relative who kept me out of her kitchen every time I visited her while menstruating (women are considered unclean when they menstruate). A male house help who ogled at my growing breasts. Men who grabbed my "pussy" while I was walking to dance class. As I neared age 18, a few well meaning relatives advised my father to arrange my marriage before it was too late, as no decent man would want to marry me.

I rebelled! I was supported by my father, who continued to push boundaries and make professionally accomplished women a new norm in our family. At 18, I left home to attend college in Massachusetts. I can only imagine the courage my father mustered to send his oldest daughter so far away. Ironically, I had chosen Mount Holyoke College, whose roots are steeped in feminist history. Mount Holyoke was founded by Mary Lyon – a pioneer in women's education whose vision was to establish institutions of higher education for women, where we could receive an education equal to that of men.

I tasted freedom! From societal expectations to marry. From sexual harassment in public spaces. From demeaning comments about my appearance. And from comments about my un-ladylike temperament when I disagreed with adults, particularly men. I learnt to be independent. I opened a bank account. I worked and earned my own income.

I learnt to drive! I chose my own career path. And I had fun at parties! I learnt responsibility. I cared for drunk friends. I spent within the income I earned. I worked overtime and saved. And I juggled deadlines.

I became political! I attended my first anti-war peace protest. I learnt about reproductive rights. I learnt about the environment. I learnt how the United States of America creates wars in other countries. I learnt how science can be misused to perpetrate grave injustices. And, I learnt how the courage of a few good men and women can foster a movement to bring freedom from slavery.

I never looked back! I went on to earn a PhD. Unlike my aunt, I married when I wanted (I was almost 30 years old) and to someone whom I chose. I had children when I was ready. And I am fortunate that despite growing up in a society that does not value women, I was supported and empowered. Education exposed me to a world of possibilities.

The challenges of sexism and misogyny in my relatively privileged world are more subtle. Getting an education is a given, and working professionally is acceptable. But marriage and motherhood still continue to be the defining identities for women. Being single or childless, whether out of choice or not, invites pity, unsolicited advice and thoughtless comparisons designed to make a woman feel bad about herself.

For those of us who have embraced marriage and motherhood, it is still expected that our partners' careers will take precedence and our primary roles will be in the home. And for those of us who are trying to juggle it all, whether out of choice or not – marriage, motherhood and work – the expectation is that we must be super humans! This means running around like headless chickens – succeed at work, cheer your child at every school activity, produce great meals, keep a clean home, help with homework. Or, be exhausted and give up something, often our careers.

While norms have shifted and it is now acceptable for women to enter the work force and juggle it all, they have not shifted for men to assume a greater share of the workload at home. While many parents like my father raised girls of my generation to be professionally ambitious, they did not raise boys to do their fair share in the home – nor did they raise boys to define their primary identities within the context of marriage or fatherhood. Boys continue to be raised with the expectation that their main role is to be a breadwinner and professionally accomplished. As one of my professors once said, "As long as norms don't also change for men to assume equal roles and responsibilities within the home, progress and opportunities for women in the professional context will continue to be hampered."

My two daughters (ages 10 and eight) are growing up taking for granted a future that I could not at their age, and that many girls their age, are still denied. Millions of girls continue to be denied opportunities to go to school, are married as children, and face innumerable hardships and abuse. Growing up in Switzerland, my daughters are fortunate to have access to a good education. Like me, they will have a choice to marry or not, and with whom and when.

They may, however, continue to face the more insidious forms or newer manifestations of sexism and misogyny. There are still subtle messages about girls not being good at Science, Technology, Engineering and Math (STEM) subjects as compared to boys, which has resulted in far fewer girls graduating in these subjects and entering related professions. Society continues to socialise girls to not assert themselves, voice their opinions or tout their achievements, whereas boys are expected and encouraged to do so. Bullying, stalking, sexual harassment and abuse, including in school, is pervasive and threatens their self-confidence. With increasing access to and the influence of media, including exposure to hyper-sexualised images of women, I worry about the potential impacts on their self-esteem. My children will grow up to be "women of colour" in a predominantly white society. I wonder how I can shape them to be resilient in the face of these multiple forms of prejudice.

One of my first bosses once said to me, "The work of achieving equality for women is a 80-year project." So, I dream that my daughters and their generation will be torch-bearers for a world in which women are equal and in which we will see greater numbers of women astronauts, scientists, engineers, mathematicians, CEOs, legislators, prime ministers and presidents. A world in which all forms of violence and abuse are not tolerated. A world where boys are raised to nurture and where men's equal sharing of the domestic workload and fathering are a norm. A world in which equality of opportunities will not be just for the privileged few (like my daughters), but for every girl, everywhere!

Avni Amin works on gender equality and violence against women at the World Health Organization in Geneva, Switzerland. She has worked on women's health and particularly sexual and reproductive health and rights for over 20 years, with a focus on Africa, Asia and the Middle East. She has a PhD in International Health from Johns Hopkins University School of Public Health. Avni grew up in India, and her feminist beliefs are influenced by what she observed growing up in a patriarchal society and by strong women in her life. She is a mother of two girls and dreams of a future when equality for women will be a given.

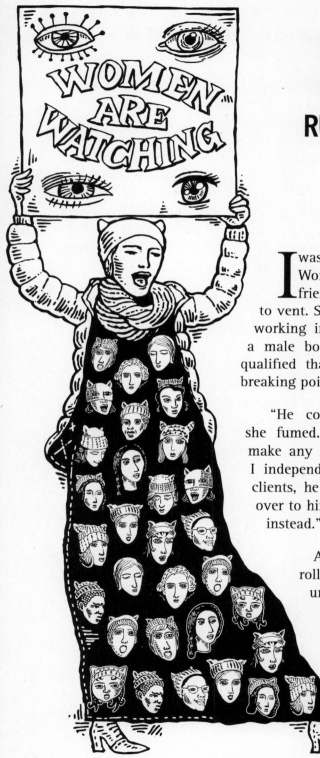

I'M SO TIRED OF MEDIOCRE MEN RUNNING THINGS

Rebecca Davis

I was on my way to Cape Town's Women's March when a close friend phoned. Aneeqah wanted to vent. She is a medical professional working in a private practice, under a male boss who is technically less qualified than her, and she was at a breaking point.

"He constantly undermines me," she fumed. "He doesn't trust me to make any important decisions, and if I independently take on high-profile clients, he demands that I turn them over to him so that he can treat them instead."

As I listened to Aneeqah, a rolling stream of flashbacks unspooled. Her words were as familiar to me as an old song. I had heard them from countless other female friends over the years. The details changed, the professions altered, but the basic facts remained constant.

Highly competent women toiling under – or alongside – men who were barely performing in their jobs, and yet continuously enjoying greater recognition and reward. Skilled, intelligent women who repeatedly endured humiliations both great and small; who were reminded in a hundred different ways a week of their inferior standing in the workplace and the world, *because they are women.*

I remembered my friend Jen, a successful woman in the male-dominated mining industry, who is constantly asked to take the minutes of meetings she attended, despite being surrounded by male subordinates.

I remembered my friend Tammy, whose male boss relies on her to manage almost every aspect of his life, and part of whose unofficial job description has become attempting to dodge his clumsy attempts at gropes and kisses while drunk.

I remembered my wife Haji, who worked for a year under a man who sought to blame her every time his own professional inadequacies were exposed by superiors.

And I remembered my own experiences, in a world which constantly seeks to teach women and girls that their place is below a man, no matter their qualifications or achievements.

I remembered being 10 years old, on a hot day in Malawi, and news reverberating around the school like a gunshot: my twin sister had defeated the reigning male tennis champion. And I remember, as if it were yesterday, the curious way that the news was reported. "Richard was beaten ... *by a girl!*" My sister remaining nameless; the focus on the bizarre, inexplicable humiliation of the rightful champion. A sense, unspoken but strong, that *this is not how things are supposed to be.*

I remembered being in an all-girls high school in Cape Town, with Matric final exams approaching. The reverence with which our male counterparts' intellectual prowess was discussed; within our mixed friend group, it being well known that Rob and Andrew were the clever ones; the ones whose exam results would guarantee them a passport to any course of study they wished. And then: the revelation upon the publication of results, that almost all the girls had done better. That we were the clever ones all along, but that it would take an anonymous, standardised exam to make that plain.

I remembered the first years of university, in Grahamstown, gritting my teeth in tutorial after tutorial as confident male students sucked up all the oxygen in the room with lengthy monologues, arguments and points of view. I remembered the suffocating frustration of knowing that I had things to say – interesting things, important things – but might never have the chance to air them. I remembered my voice betraying me, trembling when I did speak, and I remembered longing for one iota of the ease with which these boy-men considered themselves entitled to hold court.

I remembered the academic mentor I hero-worshipped, and whose approval I had craved, taking me aside at a function to drunkenly confide that he wanted to "fuck me and suck me." And I remembered how I nervously laughed it off and did nothing, absolutely nothing about it afterwards, because maybe I should be flattered by the attention of someone I so admired?

I remembered the male manager who rebuked me for not smiling enough as a waitress: an admonition never doled out to my sullen male peers. I remembered the male boss who told me that he only hired pretty women, because "they cost the same as the ugly ones."

I remembered my shock, just recently, upon realising that a male friend doing the same work as me was being paid more than three times as much.

As I listened to Aneeqah talk, on that morning of the Women's March, a quiet rage burned within me. It had been burning for some days. I am not American, and have no personal ties to the United States of America. But in the 2016 electoral defeat of Hillary Clinton, by an unqualified, sexist, racist buffoon, I felt again the searing reality of what it means to be a woman in this world.

Millions of women know, although perhaps on a tiny scale, what it felt like to be Hillary Clinton on the morning of that election result. We know it in our bones and our guts: how it feels to be passed over for the man who talks over you, who undermines you, who sexualises you, and who reminds you that whatever your accomplishments, you remain just a woman.

I had brought with me in the car that day a blank piece of white card and a thick black marker. I wanted to write upon it a slogan that somehow captured everything I was feeling, but I settled instead for expressing the very deep, weary disappointment that enveloped me that morning.

Ending the call with Aneeqah, I uncapped my marker and wrote, in block capitals: SO TIRED OF MEDIOCRE MEN RUNNING THINGS. And then I got out of the car, placard held aloft, to join the other women who had gathered to march that day. We may be tired, but we cannot afford to shut up.

Rebecca Davis grew up in Malawi and Cape Town, and was educated at Rhodes University in Grahamstown, South Africa, and the University of Oxford in the United Kingdom. She is an award-winning journalist whose writing appears in the *Daily Maverick* and a range of other South African publications. Rebecca's first book, a collection of humorous essays titled *Best White*, was published in 2015.

LE FEMMES **NASTY**

Linda Diedericks

Women won't back down
Less fear more love
Revolution of love

Women's rights are human rights
Respect my existence

Have courage and be kind

We the people
I will not have my life narrowed down to
someone else's whim or someone
else's ignorance
Love not hate makes America great

Droits Pour Les Femmes Americaines
Well-behaved women seldom make history
It's time for women to stop being
politely angry
A woman's place is in the revolution
A woman's place is in the resistance

Je suis Nasty Woman
We should all be feminists
Grab patriarchy by the balls
Do not normalise this
Stay outraged

My body, my choice
Ne touche pas my pussy
Silence is not an option

Women will not be
trumped upon
The future is still female

Linda Diedericks has spent much of her working life in the civil society sector, primarily in the community grant-making sector at established development organisations such as Social Change Assistance Trust and Hivos South Africa. She holds an Honours Degree in Gender and Transformation from the University of Cape Town. In 2005, Linda completed a Masters Level Course on Cross Sector Partnerships at Cambridge University. She is a Senior Policy Officer of Political Affairs at the Embassy of the Kingdom of the Netherlands in Pretoria, has an interest in philosophy and has attended short courses at the Practical School of Philosophy. Linda has a love for poetry as a way of dealing with life and its complexities, as well as reflecting on the world in which we live. The ability to write what she pleases and to express herself through the written word transports her into an artistic, creative space where her imagination can run wild and be free from judgement.

OH, NO YOU CAN'T GO TO HEAVEN IN A BROKE DOWN CAR[37]

Anastasia Slamat

The first feminist I came to know was 14 years old. I met her at church – let's call her 'Christine' for the purpose of this story. Having started our first period, we were both volunteered to pledge a purity promise to God.[38] We were told how beautiful sex was – a gift from God to be shared between husband and wife, and described as the "best gift you can give to your husband." We were told that no man wants to marry a woman who has had many partners. We were told that we should aspire to be like Sarah of old, faithful and obedient and the Lord will reward you with a good man. Don't you want to get married?

When we took the oath, a sonorous voice from the front of the room asked one of the congregation members to hush the boys playing on the church veranda. We were asked whether we had any questions regarding what was taking place. We were informed that this was, after all, a space where we could voice our concerns without fear of rebuke. Christine proceeded to ask why the boys, who were our age, were playing outside and were not here, taking this vow with us. I thought to myself, "What is wrong with her?" Why does she insist on making this beautiful occasion awkward? Why couldn't we just get on with the ceremony?

The boys were not taking the vow because this was the way things were done. We were told, "You ladies have an extremely important job to keep your bodies pure. Men are naturally lustful and lack self-control, and therefore it is up to you to guard your temple. *Hulle is maar net mansmense.*"[39]

The ceremony was attended by predominantly older and married women who clucked together afterwards, to discuss what had just ensued. "She's a funny one, that Christine – showing off and looking for attention in an ostentatious display of rebellion. She will never get married." These were the sorts of comments directed at Christine who had gumption enough to question the ceremony.

Christine moved to Pretoria with her parents, but I would never forget her. Her question stirred deep parts of the 12-year-old me. In a fit of self-loathing, I thought of her when I broke my purity vow. I thought of how many "sluts" were also sitting on their bedroom floors, tortured by guilt and mourning the loss of their sacred hymens.

In our community, older women, the avatars of piousness, wielded an immense amount of power. They had a role in interpreting the Holy Book and subsequently prescribing sexual ethics onto the bodies of younger women and girls. "Sexual ethics" or my personal favourite, the term "religio-moral absolutes," ultimately dictate the lifestyle choices of women and girls on a daily basis.

My years of unfurling were by no means easy. I internalised the way in which the church policed women's bodies and without being aware of it, I policed my own body. When I was old enough to consume alcohol, I only drank red wine because it resembled the wine served in Holy Communion.

I never made big decisions without seeking male counsel.

I saw bad occurrences and failures as God's wrath, punishment for my disobedience and impurity.

I experienced similar onslaughts of patriarchy at school. Girls were asked to assemble in the school hall for a talk on teenage pregnancy and abstinence, while the boys, absolved of any responsibility, were told to play soccer instead. I learnt very quickly that my sexuality was my most prized possession as a woman. It was the most I could possibly offer a man.

By assuming the roles of sexual gate-keepers in relationships, young boys are free to adopt and maintain a relatively unrestrained approach to sexuality and relationships. It is the girls who have to wear the mantle of responsibility, who have to be good, who have to ensure that they don't have an "accident." This responsibility weighed on me, and I recall counting down the days to my next period, knowing full well what it would mean if I had a child "out of wedlock." I would be damaged goods. I would have to formally inform the church minister of my current "state" and be placed under *tug en vermaan*.[40] What would people say?

Many things weighed on me after Christine ignited my feminist flame. The concept of slut shaming weighed on me. Having my movements restricted, always accompanied by a male (to protect me with his privilege, of course) weighed on me. The monitoring of my behaviour by my school, my church, my community, my government, my media, weighed on me. And the use of shame to constrict me, to force me into compliance, angered me.

It was not until the second semester of my first year at university, attending a course on gender studies, that I possessed the right verbiage to describe the heaviness I have carried for years. The patriarchy enforced by various structures was force-fed to me. I digested it; I internalised it.

In one of her TED Talks, one of my favourite African writers, Chimamanda Ngozi Adichie, describes her definition of a feminist as someone who says "Yes, there is a problem with gender as it is today and we must fix it, we must do better." I agree. We must do better for ourselves and our next generation of girls. We must teach them bravery to deconstruct the notions of patriarchy and misogyny. We must teach them that sex is neither shameful nor wrong. That sex is not the only valuable thing to offer in a relationship. That shame loves and thrives on secrecy.

Anastasia Slamat is a junior political consultant at a Cape Town-based consultancy. She holds Bachelor, Honours and Masters Degrees in International Relations from Stellenbosch University, majoring in Political Science and Gender Studies, and has a keen interest in social justice issues, state feminism, local sites of agenda-setting for grassroots women and public policy. Anastasia has worked on local, national and international projects, including local municipality research and consulting, business advisory services in conjunction with South Africa's Department of Trade and Industry and country risk analysis for the German Federal Government. She has also contributed to drafting AgriParks (national rural economic development project) masterplans, and served on the Secretariat to the High Level Panel on Assessment of Key Legislation and Acceleration of Fundamental Change.

RUMBLING SPLASHES

Vuyiseka Dubula

Echoes of childhood, no one
listening to the soft humming
No mark of the lyrics she was singing,
pain engraved all over her face
Sounds clumsy in a methodical
and melodious rhythm
Her sounds race with the dark
sounds of a drumming well
Sounds of childhood, no one paying attention to the salient drone

Her pain and yearning for mama's rescue vibrates in her song
The city chaotic, noises of an abusive father daze the melody
Her melody draws power from the valley below the Dutywa Hills
Childhood memories of passing cattle soothe her song
Secure her like a rain drop captivating a stint to dry earth
Yet her sounds compete with the drumming of the dark well

Sounds of childhood, no one listening to the soft humming
The vivid memories of that awful touch from a father
Ending with a piece of cloth thrown on the floor
Everything in that small body numb for so many years
No amount of eyes closing or pleading takes the pain away
Tears turn into a lifetime waterfall,
sounds of the city smother her cry

Rumbling splashes below echo her call for freedom
Every day hoping, she lives for a rubber to undo her experience
She hates him abundantly and wishes for a stray bullet on him
Sounds of her childhood, coming in all directions
Like mountains spitting out a waterfall, a mess
In time the splashes are collected, the monsters disappear
But, sounds of many others are a constant reminder
That it all begins at home and no one
listens to the melody

57

Vuyiseka Dubula is currently completing her PhD at the Centre for Civil Society at the University of KwaZulu-Natal. Her post-graduate studies were focused on HIV/AIDS management in the workplace. Vuyiseka has been involved with the Treatment Action Campaign in multiple roles since 2001, and as the General Secretary (Executive Director) for eight years. She joined Sonke Gender Justice as Director of Policy and Accountability in 2014, and is currently the Director of Programmes. Vuyiseka also has experience in academic postgraduate teaching and student supervision in her lecturing role on social aspects of HIV/AIDS, at the University of Stellenbosch Africa Centre for HIV/AIDS Management.

FEELINGS BE DAMNED:
THIS IS WORK

Berenice Paulse

I stood accused of being too emotional.

It was not the first time either; after all, how many women who have had the audacity to use their voices have not been accused of this? I have had my fair share of "too emotional" over the years, starting as a young girl who dared to challenge the constraints of patriarchy. Over the years, it has invariably been blamed on my hormones, pre-menstrual syndrome, my womb, and lately, menopause.

This time around, however, the indictment was accompanied by an unbridled display of hostility and aggression. It happened at work. The person who accused me of being too emotional was having a meltdown. He was screaming at me in rage, towering over me in an attempt to intimidate. He wanted what he thought he was entitled to, and no amount of explaining or reference to policy and procedure would appease him. He was furious, felt entitled to his fury, and felt justified in unleashing it on me.

My feelings oscillated between shock, horror, incredulity, violation, shame, and eventually my own anger. In the aftermath of such unchecked rage, all these emotions surged through me, but outwardly, I remained calm. I brushed off the concern of my peers. It did not matter that I was shaking on the inside; I was determined to, at least on the outside, appear composed and unruffled. I was determined to stay behind my desk the full day and tick tasks off of my to-do list. The consummate professional. Why was that so important?

When we met the following day with a manager (who happened to be a woman) in an attempt to mediate, my male colleague charged that I was "just too emotional," and proceeded to list previous occasions of my supposed emotional indiscretions. One of these was when I told colleagues I was "very disappointed" in a decision taken by the majority. The irony was completely lost on him. Here we were because he had had a meltdown, but it was my problem. In fact, he apologised for what he termed his "outburst" the previous day. Still, I was the one being too emotional. I asked myself, "Are testosterone-fuelled outbursts by definition not emotional then?"

This incident reminded me of one of my earliest interactions with the same colleague when I, as his immediate manager, suggested changes to a document he had drafted – which he blatantly ignored. Having reviewed his final draft, I called him to enquire whether he disagreed with my comments, since he had failed to implement any of the suggestions. Instead of giving me a straight answer, his instinctive response was to dig into the time-honoured patriarchal bender, "Well, if I knew you were going to be so emotional about it, I would just have done it!" I was flabbergasted. I called him out on his inappropriate response a few days later, but I took my time about it – I was advised to be very calm, read "not emotional," when I dealt with the issue. Lo and behold that we should ever utter the phrases "I am angry", "I am disappointed", "I am displeased" at work.

These, and other, experiences underscore how, as women, no matter how rational one's argument, or compelling the reasoning, it is easy to dismiss, ridicule and belittle whatever we say under the misogynist standard of being "too emotional." We saw it during the US elections, when a television journalist interviewed a middle-aged woman from middle America about Hillary Clinton's chances of victory, which the woman dismissed because Clinton as a woman would be "too emotional" to rule a country. This message was recently reinforced in South Africa, when the ruling African National Congress' Women's League decided to bolster its presence at its fifth national policy conference with six men, because it was reported by the media that women's voices tended to be "too emotional" during debates.

"Too emotional" remains a weapon of choice to silence non-complacent – or in the world of Trump and his misogynist compatriots – "Nasty" Women. As a gag instrument, it is universally accessible, frequently invoked, and can be used indiscriminately without fear of retribution. Because society, including some women, has bought whole-heartedly into the false cultural dualism of rationality and emotion, emotion has come to be associated with negative connotations. It is shameful, unwanted, undesirable. On the other hand, rationality is its appealing twin, highly sought after, actively pursued. Its Latin origin, *rationalis*, means reasonable or logical. Since emotion has been designated the evil twin, it therefore stands to reason (pun intended) that it has been consigned to the social margins by patriarchy, declared irrefutably "feminine."

Patriarchy, however, continues to rely on and benefit from our emotional labour in the private sphere. Societal expectations of women being "too emotional" are used to justify why we are better caregivers in the home and community. This labour is largely unpaid, exploited and undervalued, but within this context, we are allowed to have, and show, much emotion in public and communal spaces. Men, of course, are the primary beneficiaries of women's unpaid emotional labour. Women are still tasked with primary responsibility of care for the young, sick and infirm, arranging (and remembering) anniversaries, family traditions, and significant religious and cultural occurrences.

Like so many women around the world, I found myself personally invested in Hillary Clinton's 2016 US presidential campaign, intent on witnessing the shattering of what Clinton herself referred to as "the highest, hardest glass ceiling." Throughout her campaign, Clinton was dogged by indictments about her aloof and cold (read "not emotional") public persona, an accusation not levelled against her male opponents. (The unvoiced public narrative thus being that it is somehow an aberration for women not to wear our hearts on our sleeves.) The political gurus, however, were intent on wringing a speck of emotion from Clinton, her public appearances and speeches meticulously scrutinised for any hint of it.

As I watched the television commentary immediately following Clinton's concession speech, I experienced a mounting sense of discomfort. I realised that her speech, as powerful as it was in its entirety, would be the big emotional payoff. Described by some as a speech intended to spur the process of healing and reconciliation after a particularly contentious (and "vicious") election campaign, its significance was wasted on the commentators. Clinton, in her speech, called on her supporters to cherish the values enshrined in the Constitution of the United States of America, and to respect the rule of law. She spoke about a collective campaign, which in her words "was never about one person." Nevertheless, in the end, it was her admission that her loss to Donald Trump was "painful and it will be for a very long time," with the accompanying catch in her voice, which grabbed headlines.

The immediate reaction of most of the US political experts and media houses commentating on the speech was to disregard the tone and power of Clinton's concession speech, in favour of emotion. This theme also became embedded in all post-election commentary. Why the obsession with Clinton's emotion, or the lack thereof? Why were commentators gleefully vindicated by Clinton's display of emotion? Because despite her presidential ambitions, to many men and women across the globe, Hillary Clinton is, first and foremost "just a woman." Patriarchy, having relegated emotions to the feminine, was finally vindicated. It mattered that Clinton, one of the most accomplished and knowledgeable women on foreign policy and geopolitics, finally succumbed to patriarchy's expectations of how a woman should behave. That it was a warped image, distorted by patriarchy's own enslavement to dualism, hardly mattered.

Hillary Clinton's election campaign underscored, yet again, women's predicament when it comes to emotion. On the one hand, there is the expectation that we should be emotional (but not too much so that it causes embarrassment or discomfort to those around us), while on the other hand, women who are not overtly emotional also cause unease because it is considered 'unnatural.' Then there are the confines of where, as women we are allowed to express what we feel, and the societal benefits derived from our emotional labour.

The fury expressed by my colleague also exposed to me the extent to which I have come to internalise these confines; policing myself about where and how I could express my feelings. Why did I not acknowledge my myriad of emotions on the day of my colleague's meltdown? Why was it so important to appear unruffled by the verbal assault? Why would I not say that I felt violated? Why did I police my own feelings?

When I think about it, perhaps I was intimidated by the knowledge that as a woman, like so many other women, whatever I say or do (regardless of its significance or relevance), often gets lost in the "too emotional" narrative. I was possibly unwilling (afraid? intimidated? cowardly?) to bolster the false dichotomy between feeling (women) and thinking (men). In order to be taken seriously, to be respected at places of work, we often school ourselves not to "feel" or expose our feelings to others.

Even when we feel exhilarated or excited about a project or an achievement, we tend to mask it behind a bland professional persona, or we only give expression to it in a supportive (usually more intimate) space. I have witnessed male colleagues pump a triumphant fist in the air when something goes well. I have also seen male colleagues despondent at times, and I've witnessed the public meltdown of another. Yet, I find myself policing my own feelings when I had every right to feel the way I did – and I have weathered countless charges of being too emotional both at work and in my personal life. This is the backlash of the "too emotional" propaganda machinery waged against women.

With hindsight, I realise that not only are emotion and reason not mutually exclusive, but feelings are valuable and essential – this is what makes us human. And there certainly is space for it in organisations, institutions and the public realm. Our role as feminists is to undo the false narrative that assigns emotion to gender, and destabilise the construct of cultural dualism, which seeks to devalue feelings. Finally, our determination to shatter the "elusive" glass ceilings must be matched by our commitment to challenge corporate climates that serve as barriers to women's entry, organisational compatibility and advancement. As feminists, we are duty-bound to splinter corporate cultures steeped in patriarchal values and behaviours, often given expression through styles of communication, socialisation and leadership.

And by the way, the next time I am faced with emotional bullying at work, I will not shake it off like a bad cold. Faced with patriarchy or misogyny, I will not be calling it "inappropriate" either, I will tell it like it is.

Berenice Paulse is a former small-town farm labourer, who currently works as a researcher. She writes on social justice and matters that cannot, strictly speaking, be labeled party-political (given her day job), although she is often tempted to do just that. Berenice's strong views on patriarchy and the nexus between language and power has sometimes made her the object of misogynist vitriol.

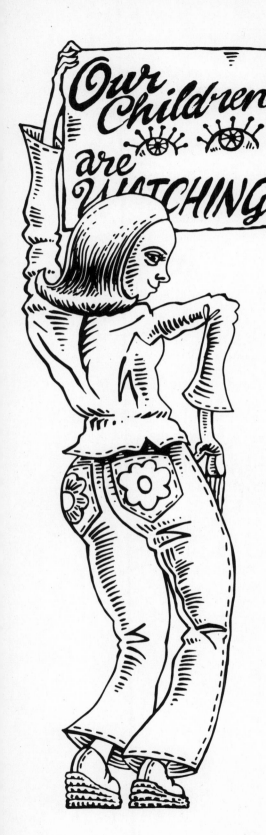

ODE TO A NASTY WOMAN

Friederike Bubenzer

(I thought you were nasty:)
You laughed the loudest.
I thought one didn't do that.
The others didn't.
Your lipstick was bright and red.
The others noticed.
You stood with the men at the
braai and drank beer.
The others didn't.
You embraced life empathically.
The others stared.

(Then I saw you:)
You opened our eyes to injustice.
The others didn't.
You believed in equal rights for all.
The others teased me.
You spoke about sex.
The others cringed.
You had more books than clothes.
The others didn't.
You were confident and bold.
The others doubted.

(Then I heard you:)
You debated politics at dinner tables.
The others were silent.
You told dirty jokes.
The others didn't.

You argued with tenacity.
The others feared you.
You believed vehemently and stood your ground.
The others listened.
You taught us manners and respect.
The others noticed.
You contested narrow minds.
You ignored the price.
You married out of love.
You stayed in love.

(Then I became you:)
You exemplify courage.
You demand respect.
You lead by example.
You personify strength.

Now your daughters are Nasty Women too.

Friederike Bubenzer is a peacebuilding practitioner who works with policy makers, civil society leaders and activists on finding ways to conceptualise and implement sustainable social justice and reconciliation processes in Africa. She is currently Senior Project Leader in the Justice and Peacebuilding Programme at the Institute for Justice and Reconciliation in South Africa and focuses on exploring the nexus between mental health and peacebuilding. She is the co-editor of the book *Hope, Pain and Patience: The Lives of Women in South Sudan* (Jacana, 2011) and holds a Masters in Philosophy in Development Studies and Social Transformation from the University of Cape Town, and undergraduate degrees in International Relations from the University of Stellenbosch. Friederike is a fellow of Columbia University's Institute for the Study of Human Rights' Association for Historical Dialogue and Accountability.

DIARY OF AN INDIAN WOMAN

Aarti Narsee

"I got married at 22 years old ... In those days they couldn't keep a girl for too long. Once they reached the age of 17, they had to get married."

My immediate reaction was anger and rage. "Um, I'm sorry ... what did you say?!"

But this is my mother's lived reality. Back then, getting married after the age of 17 meant that a girl's "sell by date" had long expired. My mother believes she would have been married off at a much younger age if it wasn't for her brother eloping with a woman of an unfavourable caste.[41]

"I got a bad name; people thought I would do the same. For a few years there were no marriage proposals. I stayed in a rural village, so city boys didn't want to marry girls like us because we were uneducated," she says.

But, eventually, after a long wait, a proposal came along.

"It was an arranged marriage. You couldn't date the boy or go out with the boy you were marrying. You only got to see him in person once. Look, I had to listen to my parents, I couldn't say anything. Those times were different."

"Once?? You got to see him once?!" My jaw dropped in shock. I can barely commit to buying anything valuable after seeing it once, never mind a new husband! The year is 2013, I was 22 years old. Fresh out of university, I had scored my very first job as a print journalist. Marriage? Not even a thought. Luckily my mother and I were on the same page.

In my early days of journalism I began writing about women's rights issues. I wrote about sexual harassment, domestic violence, rape and forced marriage. I came across such heartbreaking tales, that I still carry them with me today. So many young girls are violated by those meant to love them.

Over the course of my career as a journalist, I have come to discover that while so much has changed for women, beneath the surface, so much remains unchanged. On paper women have so many rights, but in reality these rights are just that, words on paper.

My mother grew up in a rural village called Kholvad, in India. It was here that she was exposed to the burdens of being a woman. Imagine the trickling blood of your first period flowing through a river as you wash your own clothes. Forget the idea of sanitary pads.

"Our parents never sent us anywhere alone because we were girls. They were very strict ... we were not allowed to wear dresses, or trousers. Our bodies had to be covered."

So much of my mother's childhood rings true for me too, even though I grew up in a different time. As a young girl, I was often made to dress conservatively because I was "a girl." I was not allowed to stay out late at night, unlike my brothers who had the freedom to do anything. But how could my parents have known better? This is what they were taught by their families, and society at large.

Independence was a stranger to my mother. Her first interaction with independence was after her marriage failed and she moved with her family to Zimbabwe. She doesn't like sharing the story of why her marriage didn't work out. Perhaps this is because she was told that divorced women are "tainted." You must understand, divorce amongst Hindus was always frowned upon and Hindu women bare the burden of this stigma. So all my mother says on this subject is that "he had someone else." As a young bride, she was forced to do household chores with her mother-in-law, while her husband often went away on "business."

"I had to become a different person. It felt great to earn my own money and help my family, and I learnt a lot of things at my job as a sales lady. I learnt how to manage accounts and take stock ... It was a great experience to learn so much. I didn't know how to speak a word of English when I got to Zimbabwe."

Her independence after divorce did not last for long though, because she soon married my father. I ask her if she ever thinks about what her life could have been. What if she were given the opportunity to study, and did not get married at such a young age? Or if she chose not to marry for a second time? She doesn't dwell on this too much.

But I do. My imagination runs wild.

Let us imagine that my mother went to college and had the same opportunities as her brother. Imagine if she had said "NO!" to the arranged marriage, defying her family. Imagine if she had chosen a career instead.

I believe that I am the product of my mother's imagined reality. I am the culmination of everything that my own mother could not achieve. Perhaps some might say that it's a generational thing. She did grow up in a different country, during a different time, after all.

I say "NO!"

This is a vicious cycle. One in which women are still sold off to the highest bidder. One in which women are not given the same opportunities as men. One in which women are still cat-called and sexualised by men in higher positions.

My mother is now 56 years old. She became a widow when she was just 45. The years after my father's death were probably the most trying for her, but independence is now a permanent part of her life.

Sadly, things have not changed for other young girls or women in my mother's village. Girls are still seen as a burden, and they are still not being educated. And you might believe that traveling over 8,000 kilometres to South Africa would change things. But you would be wrong. South African women face the burdens of soaring rape rates, a failed justice system, and abuse by politicians who make empty promises.

If a time capsule existed, and I could change the past, this is what would change: We need to change the way that men think. Easier said than done, right? Start with changing the minds of young boys and girls. My eight-year-old nephew is already saying things such as, "You cannot do this because you are a girl."

The only way a girl knows that inequality is not okay is if she is taught about empowerment. My mother was always submissive to her circumstances. She found no fault with the life she lived because she didn't know any better. I, on the other hand, was the complete opposite. I was exposed to the reality that women can do everything and anything.

People underestimate the important role a family can play in developing character. Parents need to learn that their daughters are worthy. They need to believe that their daughters are capable of being the leaders of tomorrow. Undermining the rights of women is a vicious cycle, and my mother and grandmother are proof of that. I was the first to break this cycle. But the reality is that many women cannot.

Aarti Narsee is a journalist based in Cape Town, South Africa. She has a passion for reporting on women's rights, justice and stories about children, and is often the youngest journalist in newsrooms and other social circles. She started off her career in print at *The Times* and *Sunday Times* in Johannesburg and then made the move to broadcasting, as a reporter at eNCA. Aarti is a Chevening Awardee for 2018/2019 and is off to study her Masters in Gender, Policy and Inequality at the London School of Economics. She has worked closely with many civil society organisations, covering topics that require the greatest sensitivity. Aarti is most passionate about creating awareness and making noise about the manner in which rape is handled in South Africa. She hopes that through her writing and reporting, she can play a role in breaking down patriarchy and rape culture.

WALKING TALL, WALKING TOGETHER

Jen Thorpe

In 2017, I had the privilege of attending two writing residencies outside South Africa, one in the United States and one in France. I spent three months writing and a fourth month travelling. I spent time in New York and Paris, all in the same year, which for a small-town person like me is pretty incredible. I felt like I was living the dream.

At the same time, I felt like I was living *in* a dream, and soon I would have to wake up and return to reality.

During these writing residencies, I made a point of going for a long walk every day. In Johnson, Vermont, in March, the average temperature was sub-zero, and the coldest it got was minus 24 degrees Celsius. Sometimes the road was frozen and the moisture in my eyes and nose would freeze, feeling like small pinpricks inside my body. On one occasion, I slipped hard on a frozen stretch of road and lay there for a while, stunned and

71

winded before I was able to walk again. There was nothing that could stop me from going for a walk.

One week in Marnay-Sur-Seine, in the north of France, temperatures were above 30 degrees Celsius. The clouds rolled in, threatening to cool the air down, then hovered over us for hours, preserving the humidity and making it feel even warmer than it was. As I walked swiping my hands in front of my face like an amateur boxer, horseflies bit at me and small gnats buzzed constantly around my face. It didn't matter what the insects wanted with me, I walked.

I walked these walks, even when I didn't want to, even when I was tired. Even when it was freezing, or raining, or the sun was beating down on my shoulders so hard that I thought I might boil over. I walked. I walked for all the walks that I can't take at home because I am too scared. I walked like my life depended on it.

Between these two trips, I returned home for two months of work. On the very first day back, I went to visit some old colleagues. Walking down the street towards their office, I was sexually harassed by a man walking slightly behind me. I crossed the street to get away from him, but he persisted, moving into the middle of the road and leering at me – making comments about my appearance, asking me to talk to him, and saying hello over and over again until hello felt like a threat. He whistled and licked his lips. I walked faster. He didn't stop.

When I turned and screamed at him to leave me alone, a second man sidled up to walk beside me, telling him to go away. He finally left me alone then. My knight in shining work suit said, "You shouldn't get so worked up," smiling proudly at his modern-day chivalry.

I was torn between rage and relief. Between swearing at him that he shouldn't feel so proud to rescue me, in a world where he didn't also tell the harasser what he was doing was wrong and rather made it seem like I was "his" woman – and being grateful that at least the man harassing me had stopped, and the imminent danger of my situation had dissipated. I hated that my only options on this short walk were anger, gratitude or fear.

That day, I read a line from Kholeka Putuma's poem *Memoirs of a Slave and a Queer Person*.[42] It was only one line, but it knocked me in the chest, and broke through the hard façade of anger that we all wear to survive as women in South Africa. Kholeka writes, "I don't want to die with my hands up or legs open."

It shook me awake.

As women in South Africa, we don't feel safe in our homes, in our cars or taxis, in our buses or Ubers, on the street, in bed with someone, in our schools, in public, or in ourselves. Our most common bedfellow is fear.

Putuma's poem reminded me that while we are modifying our own behaviours as women – crossing the street to feel safer, policing our own outfits and safe spaces, protecting ourselves from what feels like almost certain eventuality – we are not living. Or at best, we are living a half-life.

*

In February 2017, the unbelievable happened. And perhaps, it was the inevitable. Donald Trump was elected president. He was elected after video evidence showed him bragging about sexual harassment, after women had reported that he had sexually harassed them, and after we saw in debate after debate that he was not willing to listen to women, even if it meant he could frame his argument against them better.

This signified to all of us that people are okay with women being treated this way. In fact, Americans placed someone who did this in one of the most powerful positions in the world. Women in the USA and around the world were, I feel, metaphysically affected by the confirmation of what we had always known: the world is just fine with our suffering.

It took the ascendance of a pathological chauvinist narcissist to the head of the White House to make the world realise that something has gone horribly wrong. As complaints, critiques and emotions spilled across the news and social media, my first reaction was to remind everyone that in South Africa, we had already been living with a pussy-grabbing president for the previous eight years. We watched a rape trial against our then-president fail miserably, allowing patriarchy to squash a woman and send her into hiding. We have watched other women prop violent men up to gain power for themselves.

But what I really wanted to say was that time would not make this appointment feel any easier. Time makes it only more difficult. Because after a while, statements and actions like those from these two chauvinists are only further normalised, and then it becomes harder to convince people that they are wrong.

Now we have a new president in South Africa, and for a moment in early 2018 things felt hopeful. After all, this was the man who had lead SANAC and pushed for policies in support of women. In his first State of the Nation Address he argued that we can't be free in South Africa until women are free. And yet, in July 2017, I watched a video clip of President Khama of Botswana giving a speech at the Southern Africa Development Community (SADC) meeting in Swaziland.[43] In his speech, Khama commented that it was unusual for both the president and deputy president of a single country to attend an event outside their country at the same time, a reference to the fact that both the president and deputy president of South Africa were in attendance that day. As Jacob Zuma cackled at the table, Cyril Ramaphosa laughed somewhere in the audience. The source of their laughter was explained by President Khama's next comment:

> But, when Cyril Ramaphosa heard that there was going to be a cultural event, that involved hundreds and hundreds of young Swazi maidens, he said to President Zuma, "On this occasion you are not going alone."

It was funny because the president of Botswana suggested that South Africa's then deputy president (in his 60s) had flown to a regional meeting of the heads of Southern African states – on tax-payers' money – not because he was needed, but because there was an opportunity to watch half-naked underage girls dance.

To me, it wasn't funny at all.

In March 2018 our new president, a potential champion for women's rights, appointed a Minister of Women whose own failure to lead her department has, on several occassions, almost deprived South Africa's poorest citizens, many of whom are women, of their social grants. Some have likened this appointment to a presidential middle-finger at over 50 percent of the population. You'll have to forgive me if I'm reticent to accept his requests that we "send him."

*

I don't know a single person in South Africa who doesn't know at least one woman who has been raped. When I tell this to people who don't live in South Africa, they are quite literally, speechless.

In South Africa, we hear about rape every single day. We watch news reports of lesbian women raped and murdered in homophobic acts of violence, of sex workers murdered by famous artists just because they could, of poor women abducted and trafficked while searching for a job. We hear stories of abuse from our neighbours, friends and family members, if we don't know these stories ourselves.

We see and we hear, and we see and we hear, and at some point we just switch off and go about our business – until the next time we have to scream at a stranger in the street and the adrenalin kicks in, and the sound and sight of it all comes rushing back like a tidal wave of emotions and we can't pretend any longer.

One summer day, after being sexually harassed twice in one year by two separate colleagues and reporting one of these incidents to my workplace that was not resolved despite following formal processes,[44] I walked into work and the wind blew strong and my skirt blew up, ever so slightly.

Hand at the ready, I stopped it.

A police officer guarding the entrance observed this with a mischievous grin, and as I walked by, he said to me, "Next time don't hold it down."

On that day, I screamed at a man with a gun.

The worst thing about it? I felt lucky that he didn't do anything with it.

This is not a life. We are not living. We are doing something that's closer to getting by.

*

In 1956, more than 20,000 South African women came together, across race and class, and marched in protest against the required extension of passbooks for women. In South Africa, we commemorate this event each year on 9 August when we celebrate Women's Day.

*

The truth is that legally in South Africa, we have it better than in the United States and many other "progressive" "developed" countries. If you're into it, you will know that our law is some of the best on the planet for promoting gender equality. Our Constitution is one of the slickest, most liberal, pieces of legislation in the world. It tells me that I can choose what to do with my sexual and reproductive health, and I shouldn't be discriminated against because of my sex, gender or sexual orientation. It creates a commission that is supposed to protect the right to equality, and another to protect human rights. It says that all other law cannot continue, if it breaks these rules of promoting equality. It has my back.

Thing is, this luxurious law forgot to bring society, the people, with it.

In some sense, our law is speculative fiction. It might happen one day, if you can believe it's possible, but it's not happening just yet.

*

In 2017, some of the largest Women's Marches in history took place around the world. Estimates range from a few hundred at some marches, to hundreds of thousands at others. I looked at one photo, from the Women's March in Washington DC,[45] where hundreds of thousands of people, with their friends and family and children, marched together. At the bottom of a street lined with American flags, a poster shouts "I'm With Her", with arrows pointing away from the text and towards the edges of the poster. You can't see the person holding the poster.

They're just one tiny person. But what they were saying is, "Hey you, out there! You're not alone."

If you think these marches were against Trump or for Clinton, you are naïve. These marches were not about two rich white people.

They are about the fact that women, cisgender or otherwise, have had enough. We have had enough of narratives that position our bodies for the taking, for consumption, for men's pleasure. We have had it with wage inequality. We have had it with the gendered burden of care work, with the unequal burden of illnesses including HIV, with the lack of women's representation in boardrooms and government. We are tired of not being able to walk freely. We are tired of not owning or reaping the rewards of the economy and the land we work in and on, often for less pay than our male counterparts.

These marches showed that women are able to walk together, to take up space next to one another and to take that space back for ourselves to build our own power. They showed, like the 1956 Women's March in South Africa, that it is possible to organise across the class, gender and race spectrum. Did all of these women marching get along with one another? I doubt it. Were they saying that their struggles or experiences were the same? No. Was it equally possible for all women to march? Definitely not. These marches did not seek to erase or ignore difference; they sought to unite despite – or because of – difference. Were these marches perfect? No way. Were they necessary?

Absolutely.

They were necessary so that as women, we could tell one another that we have not given up. To send the message to patriarchs and power holders that if they keep trying to hold us down, we will not just surrender. To tell our children and each other that this situation is not normal and we should not accept it. To say that we can do this, we can change things, if we do it together.

These marches were just a moment in a long history of oppression, but they were also a moment of hope. It will remain necessary to march, and to walk together, until it is safe enough for us to walk alone.

Jen Thorpe is a feminist writer and researcher. She has written about women's rights and gender equality since 2009 on platforms including *Mail and Guardian Thought Leader*, *Women and Girls Hub*, *Women24*, and *FeministsSA*. She is the editor of two collections of essays, *My First Time: Stories of Sex and Sexuality from Women Like You* (Modjaji, 2012), and *Feminism Is* (Kwela, 2018) and has published a novel, *The Peculiars* (Penguin South Africa, 2016). Follow her on Twitter @Jen_Thorpe.

"I'M WITH HER"

Zama Khanyile

I'm with her. I am, because you are. Umuntu ngumuntu ngabantu.

As I reflect on the prominent posters of the worldwide Women's March on 21 January 2017, and specifically the meaning of the slogan "I'm with her," I decide to conduct a mini-survey. I want to ascertain how people interpret the words. What do my friends, family and colleagues think of this feminist phrase making its way across the USA, and the Global North? What does "I'm with her" mean to them? What does it mean to South African women, and men? And what does it mean to me?

I provide a photograph of an unknown white person holding a protest sign and ask, "What do you associate with the slogan 'I'm with her'?" Some responses make me question the levels of awareness around the Women's March, as well as its significance for the feminist movement over the past few years, in particular. Some responses make me think about our specific struggles as black women, and as South African women, in the context of the wider feminist movement. And some responses make me reflect on the rights and choices of South African women, in all of our cultures, backgrounds and places of work, love and life.

The Women's March, a worldwide protest, highlighted a plethora of women's issues and more specifically, societal issues including human rights, immigration reform, healthcare reform, reproductive rights, the natural environment, LGBTIQ rights, racial equality, freedom of religion, and workers' rights.[46] Spurred by the inauguration of United States President Donald Trump, the Women's March may have started in the USA, but it took on a life of its own and the messages resonated the world over. To me, the "I'm with her" slogan resonates as a powerful statement of solidarity amongst the women present at the march, and is a call to unite all women.

So, I am surprised to learn that only 23 percent of my survey respondents correctly identify the slogan as associated with Hillary Clinton's campaign and the Women's March. One response is, "This white woman is protesting with her mates," while another says, "White women that don't represent black women's struggles." These responses highlight a well-known issue in the feminist movement – black women frequently feel left out, left behind and underrepresented in the fight for gender equality and promotion of women's rights worldwide. We are alone in the struggle for our rights, teetering between gender discrimination and race discrimination.

The intersection between race and gender in the fight for women's rights is an incredibly real issue, particularly in the Global South. Our own political history in South Africa teaches us that black women have very specific gendered experiences, located within a history of pervasive race and class discrimination. The issues that we grapple with on a day-to-day basis are very different from those of white women, and yet the spaces in which we can confront these issues are limited to our own. Because of this, white women and women of privilege in other ways need to be allies. We need them to understand this delicate intersection, understand our nuanced issues and speak up for our rights. We need to find ways to bridge the gap between the feminist movement and black women who seek to identify with it. All of this is critical to building greater unity in feminist movements worldwide.

I'm with her. She might be Black, White, Asian or Mixed Race. She is woman, and so am I.

One interesting take on the slogan comes from a young black woman, "The person who stated this is not just with one particular person but with a crowd of women who are of different age groups. And it's interesting because it implies that the 'her' could exclude the African race." The understanding is that the implied solidarity inherently excludes African women; a reminder of how "othered" the experiences of African women are. This respondent clearly feels a sense of "otherness" between her issues as a young black woman and the issues associated with the Women's March. It makes me ponder the intersections of women's rights not only across race lines, but also across ethnicity, age, ability and sexuality. How do we build a sense of inclusivity, where everyone feels assured that we are speaking on behalf of the issues of all women?

Another young respondent alludes to how women at different ages and stages in their lives must contend with issues specific to that phase, such as girls menstruating for the first time and grappling with sexual orientation, young women getting married or having children, and older women facing menopause and the death of their partners and friends. The young woman in question decoded "I'm with her" as a message of safety and well-being for all women and girls – a united front for all of our causes and stages of life.

I'm with her. She is a child, she needs my protection.
I'm with her. She is a teenager, she needs my guidance.
I'm with her. She is a woman, she needs my support.

It is interesting how South Africa's social climate frames how women here internalise the message in this poster. How our predominant issues of concern are physical safety, education and mentorship, in that order. South Africa is one of the most dangerous places in the world to be a woman and almost daily we are outraged by the scourge of violence against women; by cases of physical assault; and by the rape and violent killings of women, mostly by familiar males and intimate partners. So, I was delighted when one of my three male respondents said this about the slogan "I'm with her: "Men playing an active role against women abuse!"

As women, we need advocates and allies, and these advocates need not only be women. In fact, if the women's rights movement only speaks to and about women, we will lose the fight. Violence against women and girls, gender abuse and intimate partner violence is a societal problem in South Africa, and not an issue that should be taken on by women alone. This was supported by the respondents who were women. One said, "I'm assuming it's meant to be a pro-women march, but it's mainly women here." (There were no men in the photograph I shared). We need men on board in the fight for gender justice, for equal rights for women, and this is an aspect of feminism for which I am very much an advocate.

I'm with her. She is a woman, I am a man. It is also in my interest to protect and promote her rights.

Funny enough, 19 percent of my respondents thought the "I'm with her" poster was a reference to promiscuity. My mind boggled. These responses were premised on an assumption that the image depicted a man holding the poster, that men are susceptible to having more than one partner, and in a heteronormative framework this partner would be a woman. "I'm with her" was understood to mean that the man was duplicitous and he had multiple women in his life. South Africa's gendered social order leads to gendered assumptions, and in addition to the ways in which we are socialised, cultural norms colour the lens through which we see the world. In South Africa, polygamy is acceptable in some cultures, sparking significant public discourse in the last 10 years as former President Zuma, and other public figures, have brought polygamy to the fore. Naturally some respondents in turn understand this image to be a statement on polygamy.

As an African feminist, where do I stand on polygamy? Should we judge women who willingly opt into polygamous marriages? This is an ongoing debate that requires frank, honest discussion within the context of human rights and cultural rights.

I'm with her. She has freedom of choice. I respect her choices.

While none of my respondents brought up the issue of representation in professional spaces, I know where I stand on the meaning of "I'm with her" in this regard. In South Africa, only 10 percent of CEO positions are occupied by women, and even less by black women. This is in stark contrast and misalignment to the country's demographics – where women make up over half of our population. How long will it take to level the professional playing field? It has already been way too long! We need a concerted and consistent effort to effect radical change at the top of the ladder. When women ascend and occupy positions of power, we must use this power to change the rules and create an environment conducive for other women to enter and thrive in business.

My personal journey in the corporate world has been sponsored by women. I am where I am because of women who knocked down doors and entered spaces occupied by men. They knocked these doors down, entered boardrooms and made sure that they created seats for other women (like me) to rightfully take our places. "Develop as we lead." This is an NGO motto that has reinforced my belief in the importance of mentorship and sponsorship for young girls. As a beneficiary of mentorship and sponsorship myself, I have a responsibility to lift others as I rise on the corporate ladder.

I'm with her. She is skilled and capable. I empower her. I promote her.

When confronted with the slogan, one respondent says, "Hmmmm ... This woman doesn't want to be alone." And why should she be alone? Men don't do it alone! There is a boys' club in most work environments, particularly in the corporate sector. As women, we too must focus on developing supportive and enabling networks, and networks within which we look out for each other.

I'm with her. She is not alone.

What I like most about the survey responses to "I'm with her" is that they raise the importance of supporting and standing up for women around us, the women in our own lives. I like that many respondents use the slogan to affirm the voices of those who participated in the Women's March and associate it with a call for unity, and for the inclusivity of women who are underrepresented or less-spoken for.

The beauty in these interpretations is that they are inherently subjective. After quizzing those around me, some respondents pose the question back to me, eager to hear how the slogan resonates with me personally. I connect with "I'm with her" because it is a powerful message, advocating unity in the face of difference, declaring that it does not matter who we are or what our individual issues are as women. We are all women. Black, white, abled, dis/abled, cis, trans, rich, poor... the list goes on. Many of our issues are similar, although we have our own stories and journeys, and we come from different contextual realities. I internalise the slogan to mean, "I may have my own issues to put on the feminist agenda, but, you know what, I also stand with her, her and her. I recognise her issues as a woman even though they may be different from mine. Her issues also deserve a place here."

Umuntu ngumuntu ngabantu!

This is a Zulu proverb that loosely means, "I am, because you are." Ubuntu, that praised South African phrase that is meant to hold us all together. One does not exist in a vacuum, and therefore as women, we cannot afford to be naïve, blind, closed-off or ignorant to the issues of 'other' women. We must realise that by virtue of us co-existing, we are all linked in some way. Her issues indirectly affect you and me as well. Although she may be different in age, colour, religion, language or financial standing, who are we as feminists if we cannot adopt the stance, "I am her and she is me?" This is not only for women to support other women, but it is a call to men, and all people, to support the women in our lives.

I stand with her – I am her ally.

I stand by her – I am her shoulder to lean on.

I stand for her – I am her advocate.

I stand before her – I am her mentor. I am her sponsor.

I stand behind her – I am her supporter.

I stand around her – I am her protector.

I am with her.

I am her.

Zama Khanyile is a qualified Chartered Accountant with an Honours degree in accounting from the University of Johannesburg. She has an uncanny affinity for figures and is well-versed in financial matters. She is a Fund Manager at the National Empowerment Fund where she leads a team of investment professionals in carrying out the mandate of improving access to capital by availing finance to Black Economic Empowered entities, maximising the economic participation of women, and supporting businesses with high job creation potential. Zama is President of the African Women Chartered Accountants' Forum (AWCA). She is passionate about community empowerment, especially that of young African women.

TAKING CHARGE

Luan Dreyden

Caitlin Moran said that if you have a vagina and want to be in charge of it, you are a feminist. But what if you're 10 years old and in charge of nothing? What if you're unaware of the fact that to be in charge of it, you'd have to fight? What if you're unaware that it could dictate your position in a relationship, your ranking in a family, your salary, how society sees you, the right to live well and, sadly, the right to live at all?

My journey started with a "grab" at the age of 10. The day that I realised that to be in charge of every part of me, I would have to fight – every day. It was the day of my "end of year" party at school. It was the end of Grade 6 (that's "standard four" to anyone over 40 reading this story). I was wearing a white dress with a tan belt and the party was, undeniably, worth losing sleep over the night before. So, when it all ended, I left school with a sense of boldness and decided to walk home rather than wait for my usual school bus. With my Tupperware of leftover cupcakes in hand, and still somewhat euphoric from the party and its merriment, I set off alone on my 15-minute walk home.

On my journey home, I had to cross the sports field of the local high school. As it was end of term, all the students and staff had left, and I climbed through the broken school gate to take advantage of the shortcut home. The school was a deserted space; a place where I would find myself helpless a few minutes later. I walked across the sports field and on reaching the school building with its graffitied walls, I suddenly heard footsteps, many of them, running through the courtyard like rats. I froze as I heard the footsteps coming closer, and that's when I saw them. Three boys, roughly my age, maybe a few years older, walking towards me, not saying a word. In that moment, I realised, they didn't have to. I had some idea of what was coming. I knew what was coming, not because I was an experienced woman of the world (being 10 and in charge of nothing), but because these were the situations that little girls were warned about. Well, to be honest, the warnings were about boys much older. Men, grown men with power (although that is indeed another nasty story for another time). But these were boys – dirty, bored, uneducated, misled little boys. Bigger than me, but still little.

Out of utter fear and sheer panic, I told them that they could have all the cakes in my Tupperware. I gave them the little purse around my neck and told them to help themselves to whatever they wanted and then, without a word, as though they had planned the entire sophisticated event, they did help themselves. Two of the boys held my arms and one proceeded with his small, juvenile and inexperienced hands to grab me. THERE.

About 300 emotions rushed through me, one of which was an overwhelming sense of sick, the urge to vomit. On realising that I looked decidedly ill, my juvenile attackers released my arms and I started to cry as a final plea for their sympathy. In contending with my tearful appeal, they got somewhat side-tracked, so I seized the opportunity and ran. I ran to the main road and despite the fact that the situation was more than obvious to anyone passing by, no one stopped to help me. Not one person. So, I just kept running. I stopped screaming as I soon realised that this was, sadly, a futile exercise. I ran all the way home – not even aware of the point at which my delinquent assailants had given up.

My hands were shaking as I opened our front door and Esther, who helped out at our house, threw her arms around me. I didn't have to say a word. She somehow knew what had happened and I have to wonder now, looking back at her intuition, where it came from and what from her own experience had informed this empathetic response. I cried in the hallway. I cried in the living room. I went from room to room, ceremoniously christening each room with my tears. When I was able to speak, I called my mum and proceeded to cry over the phone. The first thing she asked me was, "Did they rape you?" and when I said "No, but..." she said, "The bladdy shits, I'm on my way home."

While waiting for my mum to come home and fix it all, I finally made my way to the bathroom where I took off my pretty white dress, rolled it up into a ball and shoved it in the laundry basket. I threw my panties into the bin. I felt like they were as tainted as I was. I couldn't verbalise the pain, I just knew it had to be hidden. There was a sense of shame that I couldn't quite explain, a sense that I had let it happen. Why hadn't I waited for my bus? Why hadn't I taken a different route? Why hadn't I fought back in that moment? I then washed myself. THERE. Repeatedly until it hurt. At three o'clock in the afternoon, I put on my pyjamas. I decided that I was done with this awful day. I toddled into my parents' bedroom, sniffed their pillows and waited like the child that I was.

As soon as I heard the familiar screech of the garage door, I walked downstairs and relayed the story of the day's trauma to my mum. My mother, an elegant woman; a gentle woman; a God-fearing woman, used words that day that came from a place of fury and a fierce innate urge to protect me. Let's just say that those three boys were very fortunate that she didn't find them. Not for want of trying. My mum piled me into the car, pyjamas and all, and we scouted the neighbourhood looking for the boys that had done this to me.

I lost so much that day. I lost my voice. I lost my trust in men. I lost my sense of freedom, and I lost my childhood. In my young mind, boys no longer represented playmates, they were a sexual threat. I felt that in that awful moment, they had taken charge of what was mine and I could not fight back.

I decided that day, that I was, in fact, a member of the weaker sex and this sense of defeat followed me into adulthood and lived with me for long after. It was only many years later I realised that the physical violation of that day would stay with me and manifest itself in so many other ways.

It was with me when I was 22 years old, fresh out of the Cape Peninsula University of Technology, with a qualification in Language Practice. I was young and keen to make my mark on the world of publishing. So I was naturally thrilled one day when I was called for a job interview as a researcher. I was elated and held onto the bit of confidence that I had managed to summon up. I was soon to discover that this would be taken away from me yet again. In preparation for the interview, I bought new clothes, asked a friend to do my makeup and hair, and decided that the day I had lost my voice would finally come to an end. After a successful interview, I was offered the job and was taken on a tour of the company by my new manager. I was so very anxious. I walked nervously behind my manager, nodding fervently at everything she said, feeling the euphoria of success, feeling like I was back at that school party. I was finally regaining a bit of self-assurance. Then, one of the male staff members threw his head back and said to his colleagues, "Finally, some fresh meat!" He did not even try to say it out of earshot. The men laughed in response, while the women rolled their eyes. I should not have allowed this comment to derail my plans for success, but the memories of my childhood experience came flooding back, reminding me of my "place."

Time passed, and I eventually moved from publishing to teaching English classes. I was proud of the work I did, both in and out of the classroom. I loved my job. I felt that I had finally broken so many barriers, recaptured so much loss, and slowly started regaining my sense of self. I felt myself becoming stronger, as a woman; as an educator and as a leader. I felt like things were shifting. I decided to go with this, and embrace the sense of success that came with feeling confident professionally. I finally felt as though people listened. I had something worth saying. Of course, there were many sexist encounters, but mostly I managed to see the wood for the trees. Until those trees caught fire.

One day, I was going about minding my own business when I found out, to my shock and horror, that a male colleague, a direct report, earned substantially more than I did. He worked fewer hours, was on a probationary contract and did not have the same level of responsibility. I was the one responsible for managing a team, organising their schedules and running training workshops. Yet I earned 30 percent less than him. I was being bullied yet again. Not by prepubescent boys, but by a system.

I decided that my choices were to run, to cry, or to fight. For a few weeks, I did everything but fight. Walking away from my job would put me in a position of financial insecurity. But doing nothing meant that I was back there in my little white dress, with my Tupperware of cupcakes, ready to offer them up to the powers that be. It was clear to me that staying and keeping silent would be a form of flight. Thinking back, that fateful day in my childhood had followed me into relationships where men called all the shots. And then it hit me. Decades ago, on that school field, I had turned and run away, which was the only choice I had. But, when my mum got home and piled me into the car on a quest to hunt down my assailants, she was determined to fight back. In so doing, she showed me that I had a choice to not be silent. That, in fact, I could be in charge of something.

And so it was, that I asked for a meeting with my manager. I put forward my case and talked about the travesty of a male colleague earning more for doing less. I found my voice to say that either I be duly compensated, or I would leave. I couldn't believe that it was me saying all these bold things. And yet, their answer was no. And so it was, that I turned my back on them and walked away. It was my boldest move to date. I had just experienced the biggest change of my life. I did it for the little girl in me who felt that she was in charge of nothing, and that her fate was determined by others. The sense of control was euphoric, a heady experience for someone like me. The little girl in the white dress still lives in me somewhere, but she is in charge of something.

Luan Dreyden is a Language Practitioner, a teacher trainer for a UK-based company and an English teacher at the University of Cape Town's English Language Centre. She is also a Cambridge examiner. Her work and experience in teaching English to students from across the globe has exposed her to young people and their thoughts about the construction of identity, including gendered identity. This has sparked an interest in thinking about gender and women in differently situated realities and cultural contexts. Luan lives in Cape Town with her husband and son.

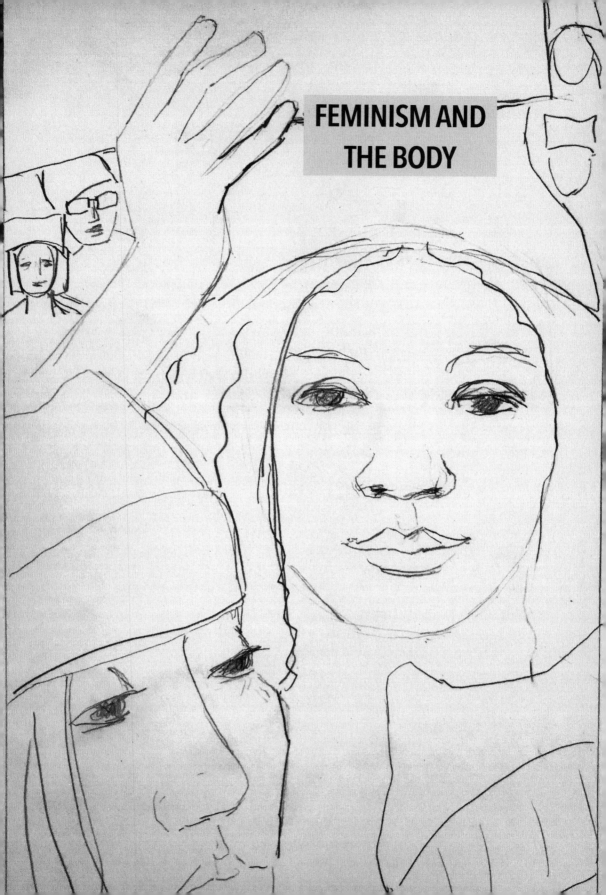

FEMINISM AND THE BODY

TO WOMB IT MAY CONCERN

Christi van der Westhuizen

It has been a most supreme act of historical subterfuge: how the patriarchal, heteronormative and racist worldview hides its obsession with the body.

Let me start my argument in the fabulous metropolis (not!) of Boksburg, nowadays an extended strip-mall strung together with other sprawling towns east of Johannesburg, known under the more aesthetic moniker Ekurhuleni. There, at the age of 17, I was sent back into the house for looking like a 'diesel dyke.' The charge and insult, signed and sealed. We – my family and I – were on our way to visit other family members. I could definitely not go in my stonewashed jeans, black lace-up boots and loose-fitting, long-sleeved shirt buttoned to the top, as per fashion at the time.

It all comes down to the body for women. Meanings are attached that will either win us kudos, or be the end of us. The kudos we will get if we are the correct size, uncovering and covering the correct amount of female flesh, with the prescribed ribbons and bows. But woe be unto us if we do not adhere to the parameters set by patriarchy's two-track mind. That day, because I had again strayed from my assigned track in the masculine/feminine division, punitive meanings were unleashed upon my young self: my (visible) gender presentation did not match my (visible) sex, so (invisible) sexuality was used as a disciplining proxy.

Recently, a Twitter troll added to the charge, this time by dragging the uterus into it. More about this later, but that is why the poster at the USA Women's March with the message "If I make my uterus a corporation, will y'all stop regulating it?" set me thinking. Multiple uses it has, the uterus. As we know, its fecundity goes beyond the obvious and mind-boggling ability to bring forth new life, in the sense that this ability is infused with patriarchal meanings to police reproduction and control women's bodies and, ultimately, our lives.

The wielding of the womb enables the hyper-embodiment of women. Women share this attribution of hyper-embodiment with working and underclass people, and black people, albeit in very different ways. It is, paradoxically, all about wresting the body from its owner. This wrest(l)ing involves language tricks. Words may be used to discipline me for how I use my body, or my body may be wielded to discipline me for the words I use. Gender non-conformism for a woman can be as simple as even daring to speak – the mere fact that I think that I may speak, whether publicly, or in work meetings, or at the dinner table at home. And these disciplinary interventions can happen at the same time, and aim to wrest from women both control over our bodies and, indeed, our subjecthood.

Even before my debut as diesel dyke, my speaking – and writing – as politicised school kid and student, and later as author and political and social commentator, has generally incensed reactionary men and women, nationalists of all stripes, and quite a number of (neo) liberals too. Heteropatriarchy spans these divides with ease. Obviously the usual hackneyed techniques are deployed to try and whip me back into the feminine line. To remind me of the tasks most suitable for my kind of body, a "big man" instructed me to make coffee for him and another "big man" in the office. Another "big man" meted out sexual harassment to remind me of the physical vulnerabilities that made me still "just a woman." Another reminded me, with hand gestures, that I met the "hour-glass" figure requirement for hetero-male enjoyment. Yet another reminded me of who calls the shots when he sidelined me professionally for starting a campaign against sexual harassment. The list goes on ...

And then there is social media, an arena for frustrated misogynists who can't get their way like they used to. They devote their existence to their Other ... like the Duracell Bunny, they repetitively and irrevocably attempt to eradicate this vexing Otherness that so depresses their jouissance[47] ... But they never quite succeed, so they keep on trying. It is an iterative process, as Judith Butler[48] taught me.

Many of these misogynists seem surprised that "ladies" nowadays are allowed to utter any words outside the home. On an obscure website it was speculated that my waywardness in speaking against patriarchy and racism was due to me not being married, as I do not have a male overseer to reprimand me. In another example, even more egregious, a generally nonsensical blog presented a photo-shopped image with my face grafted onto the body of a female bodybuilder (I wish!). Next to it, the incongruous heading read, "Don't you just love the smell of fear from female-men (sic.)?" I'm saying incongruous because, why would a "muscle Mary" (dare I) be fearful? My toothy smile in the image belied some emotions, but fear was not one of them. Nevertheless, the finger was pointed, the charge laid, the insult delivered. And Mr Blogger Man hoped that this would be a deeply distressing thought, and that the object of his prejudice would be filled with fear at the implications of her (his?) wrongness.

It was around the same time that the uterus emerged in a convoluted set of Tweets: a troll adapted a photo by scribbling Hitler's moustache below my nose, and hanging a swastika around my neck.

The charges were piled up: "femi-nazi" (cribbed from the US far-right) and "barren-wombed" lesbian. Back to the body again, like a dog scratching for an unreachable itch. Down to the womb, specifically, as a reminder that it is not only about how it is used but whether it is used that is of patriarchal concern, and both these states are drawn on to censure unruly women.

"If I make my uterus a corporation, will y'all stop regulating it?" The message making the links between regulation vis-à-vis corporations and women's bodies immediately caught my eye because too often, particularly in the South African social sciences, political economy is disconnected from gender and sex, and therefore from the body. The poster's author captures cleverly how patriarchy colludes with capitalism, how the state is used to craft opportunistic divisions between the economy and other human endeavours for differential outcomes, in which some powers are fettered and others not. In neoliberal capitalism, this collusion means that a corporation becomes a "person" under law, with rights to protect the sacred mission of accumulating profit, whatever the social and ecological costs. Deregulation is key to "free" markets. Women, on the other hand, are actual persons turned into objects in order to regulate our bodies in the service of patriarchy. Hence the continued global battle for safe abortion services, even in South Africa where abortion is legal but so stigmatised that women still die unnecessarily at the hands of unscrupulous operators. The message reminds me that decisions of regulation and deregulation produce a system: the patriarchal state in service of the patriarchal corporation and, ultimately, transnational elites of patriarchs spanning states and corporations – while simultaneously stretching long arms down to the subject, the subjective "I" who, if a woman, is policed at the level of the body.

If a womb is productive, patriarchs and their female hangers-on seek to dictate the terms of its production. If unproductive, the same coterie of bigots uses it to try and shame, in order to suppress agency. Either way, the implication is that the uterus does not belong to the person in whose body it nestles. The proprietary rights of corporations, ever expanded, stand in stark contrast to those of women. Appropriation of the uterus is mirrored in the appropriation of women's bodies, which further alienates women from our own bodies.

Women's condition can be described as a constant dispossession of the body. The dispossession of the uterus, whether we are using ours or not, is key to the dispossession of women's bodies. If this intimate part of the body – of which the use has far-reaching implications for my life – does not belong to me, then does my body belong to me? Regulation of objectified women on the basis of our uteruses is defied by women agitating for our reproductive rights, which are as much about the right to decide *how* to reproduce, as it is about the right to decide *not* to reproduce. Of course, many diesel dykes are nowadays heartily reproducing. One can just imagine the confusion that this must cause amongst the "male-men"...

Christi van der Westhuizen (DPhil) is the author of *Sitting Pretty: White Afrikaans Women in Postapartheid South Africa* (2017) and *White Power & the Rise and Fall of the National Party* (2007). She is an associate professor in Sociology at the University of Pretoria. Follow her on Twitter: @ChristivdWest

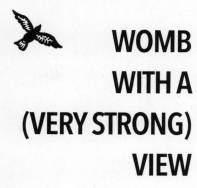

WOMB WITH A (VERY STRONG) VIEW

Helen Moffett

I am Catholic. I am infertile. I have never had a "normal" menstrual cycle, ever, and I have never had "normal" (i.e., biologically functional) ovaries.

I have never had – never needed – an abortion. Although it has always been an entirely academic question for me, I personally wouldn't have one. But this is easy for me to say, after three decades of longing for pregnancy, for a child of my own flesh and blood.

I am also a feminist. I've identified as one almost my entire adult life, although my mother says it was obvious by the time I was ten years old. I thought I was just being logical.

I cannot imagine *not* being a feminist. I am utterly at a loss when I hear "I'm not a feminist, but ..." To deny feminism, for me, means putting your hand up and saying, "I'm okay with slightly more than half the human race being considered second-class citizens. Inferior. Different. Weaker. Other."

But a secret sadness of my life has been the silence of feminist arguments and support on the issue of infertility. On related issues, like adoption; fertility treatment; miscarriage; stillbirth. I have never felt I had wholehearted feminist support or even interest in my tormenting desire to replicate my own DNA, even though it's an impulse shared with all life on this planet. But this is a subject for a different essay. Where things get "nasty" – both genuinely, and in the sense we are using it in this collection – is in the discussion of abortion, which is where all our most private and public issues of fertility, reproductive control, and bodily integrity overlap. Religion, morality, legislation, medical intervention, control, rape, incest, questions of disability – every topic and framing concept concerning abortion is fraught, contested and intensely emotional. There are faultlines, inside and outside religious and cultural groups, misunderstandings and misconceptions (no pun intended), and an enormous amount of rage and pain feeding the nastiness.

As someone affiliated with Catholic pro-choice movements, and who addressed the select committee on abortion reform in the South African Parliament in 1996, not as an expert, but to dispel the illusion that all Catholics unanimously wanted abortion to continue to be criminalised, I've spent time at the coalface of those misunderstandings. I see them repeated daily; the assumption that abortion is "legal" or "illegal" when, as in the case of all medical procedures, there isn't a country in the world that does not have legislation on terminations. (It is "legal" to have an appendectomy; this does not mean anyone is free to perform one on whoever they like, under any circumstances.) Another assumption is that all Christians, or all Catholics, consider abortion to be murder from the first day of conception – whereas Catholic hospitals have always had guidelines on whose life to save in emergencies. These make it clear that while the baby is the priority after three months of gestation, the mother's life takes priority during the first three months of pregnancy. Doctors who hold strong pro-life views are in a tricky ethical position because the precepts of medical training (to which they swear an oath of fealty) hold that the worst possible outcome for any pregnancy, at any stage, is the death of the mother – an economically active adult, who is often a parent to other children, a member of a family unit, a beloved and contributing member of society.

As any Jesuit will explain, it's a slippery slope: if abortion is permissible because pregnancy has resulted from rape or incest; the woman in question is a child herself or mentally disabled; if the foetus is malformed and has no hope of a healthy life; if the pregnancy will cost the life of the mother (which exceptions are accepted in almost all major religions that "bar" abortion or consider it a "sin"), then the question becomes one of who gets to make those decisions. And only one person, in the final analysis, has that right. Also, as someone who had friends and family members undergo illegal abortions before the reform in legislation in South Africa, I can attest that when someone you love heads off for an illicit appointment, clutching wodges of cash, you want only one thing: to see them alive again.

The pro-choice position, in my opinion, does not need defending. I want every child to be a wanted child, in a humane and caring world that does not demonise women for having sex and getting pregnant. That does not treat every conception as "immaculate" – as if no man had anything to do with the process. That is not vociferously sentimental about the rights of the unborn baby until it enters the world and needs shelter, nourishment, medical care and education, not to mention loving parenting. That does not treat women with contempt if they need the support of state welfare to raise children. That does not let fathers off the hook in every possible way: legally, financially, emotionally, spiritually. I'd like to live in a world where abortion is unnecessary. Which means that every woman needs the necessary education and freedom to make choices about her body; and access to decent reproductive health care. Deliver all of that, and then you can talk to me about closing down clinics.

*

I've always known all this in my head. A few months ago, this knowledge moved into my body. After my uterus spent several decades significantly impairing my quality of life, and then trying to kill me, it was removed. To determine what surgical procedure to follow, my gynaecologist had to perform "minor" surgery to remove the lining of my uterus – it needed to be tested for cancer, which my symptoms suggested. This was a week before I would have a five-hour anaesthetic; so the procedure (oh, what a harmless word) was done without anaesthetic. I was properly prepared. I knew exactly what would be done to me, and that it wouldn't be pleasant. I was booked in as the last patient of the day at the doctor's rooms, so that I could scream without upsetting other patients.

I could write an essay unpacking this concept alone: the knowledge that one is going to be in so much pain that silence will be almost impossible; the understanding that most women in the kind of pain that causes screaming will be anxious about upsetting others; the kindly, brutal pragmatics of it. It was explained that I would have to be driven to the surgery, and driven home again afterwards; that I could not be alone for several hours afterwards, or travel using any kind of transport unattended, because of the small risk of haemorrhage. I was given a pessary to insert ahead of time to soften my cervix, and told that it would cause cramping and pain (it did); I was encouraged to combine it with a strong painkiller. I was given permission by my doctor to wash this down with wine. I visited a lawyer to put my will in order, and spent the afternoon with a friend, who poured half a bottle of champagne into me before driving me to the doctor, and then waiting to take me home again.

My gynaecologist was soothing, competent. She talked to me throughout the procedure. Which was bloody awful. It was endurable, but only just. The only time I've been in that much pain during a medical procedure was when I needed a hollow-needle breast lump aspiration after the hospital had run out of local anaesthetic. Strapped down in stirrups, I screamed and swore, and tried to hold still. There came a time, after several minutes, when I felt I couldn't go on; my doctor encouraged and promised me it was almost over (a lie, but a necessary one).

But eventually it was indeed over; my friend took me home, laid me down and covered me with a blanket. I couldn't stop shaking. She fed me sweet tea and chocolate and offered me a bed for the night, but after four or five hours had passed, I felt strong enough to get myself home. For the next five or six days, I was in pain. This, however, was no worse than a bad menstrual period. What surprised me was the sense of violation. I felt that sucking tube, that sharp edge, inside me for days. Yet this was a neutral and necessary medical procedure. Perhaps it was my history of sexual violence that made it so traumatic.

The procedure I had was identical in every medical respect to the one that terminates a first-trimester pregnancy. As I computed this: that this is what every girl or woman who has an abortion during the first twelve weeks of pregnancy undergoes, I was overtaken by rage. Make that possessed: it brought home to me, viscerally, that any women who chooses an abortion has to undergo everything I experienced – but often first braving a chanting chorus of right-to-lifers or a sniffy nurse; intrusive medical examinations and questions; moral pontificating; outside interference in a difficult experience that should be intensely private. The notion that anyone – any member of a church or legislature – should have the right to impose their moral rather than medical concerns, to dictate to me, at that private and painful moment between me, a doctor and whatever deity I choose, makes me so angry that words fail: and that is why when I saw this poster, it spoke to me.

I lie awake wondering how a teenager, a mentally challenged woman, a rape survivor, a woman beaten down by life and bread-winning and a violent partner and the hungry mouths of other children, copes with what I now know to be the experience of early abortion. This should not be more traumatic than it already is; every woman in this position should, at the very least, feel safe.

So, to all the old white men dictating to women, the finger-wagging patriarchs who will never lie on a table with their legs apart and a knife in their guts because they cannot, at that time, bring a child into the world: fuck you very much. As long as I live, I'll fight you with everything I have.

Yours,

A Nasty Woman.

Helen Moffett is a writer, freelance editor, feminist activist and recovering academic. She has compiled three editions of a poetry anthology and a guide to academic English for Southern African students, as well as a collection of South African landscape writings, *Lovely Beyond Any Singing*. She has toured Canada with her debut collection of poems, *Strange Fruit* (Modjaji) and her second poetry collection, *Prunings* (2016), by uHlanga Press. Her collaborations include a cricket book (the late Bob Woolmer's magnum opus), the *Girl Walks In* erotica series with Sarah Lotz and Paige Nick (under the *nom de plume* Helena S Paige), and *Stray*, an anthology of animal writing for the benefit of the charity TEARS.

Helen's extensive academic work is published locally and abroad. She has a special interest in development editing and the training of young editors, writers, journalists, and researchers. Recent projects include co-editing the Short Story Day Africa anthologies *Migrations* (with Efemia Chela and Bongani Kona) and *ID* (with Nebila Abdulmelik and Otieno Owino); a memoir of Rape Crisis to mark the 40th year of the organisation's founding; and a book on Cape Town's water crisis. She blogs at www.helenmoffett.com.

THOUGHTS ON RAPE, RACE AND RECONSTITUTING SUBJECTIVITY

Rebecca Helman

I am struggling to remain afloat amidst increasingly public and publicised violence against womxn.[49] As white men lead the backlash against the minds and bodies of black people, queers and womxn, I am simultaneously furious and despairing. The imperialist-white-supremacist-capitalist-patriarchy[50] is under my skin, in my lungs, wrapped around my throat. Some days I cry, other days I write. Often I do both.

In writing about my own experiences of trauma, violation and fear, I am trying to make sense not only of what has happened to me, but also of the many tangled threads that bind my experience to those of others. My thoughts are only partly formed, often conflicting and contradictory. I hope they are the beginning of something more, something hopeful.

*

When I was 21, I was at a party where two womxn were raped. They had gone for a walk just down the road from the party. When they did not return, some of us started to worry. We sent a group of people to look for them. As I waited on the dark patio, with my hands clenched in tight fists, I knew something terrible had happened. I waited, with the other guests, for the specific nature of the terribleness to be confirmed. Eventually someone came running out of the darkness towards where we anxiously waited. He took a breath and clutched the wall of the patio. "The worst has happened," he gasped, "they have been raped."

Almost five years later, as I was dragged by a man towards a secluded patch of bushes, I thought to myself, "It is about to happen, the worst thing, the thing I have always feared. I am about to be raped."

Following my rape, I have endured many gasps and shudders as I disclose what happened. Some womxn say directly to my face that being raped is their worst fear. Others write long statuses about it on Facebook. All of these responses remind me that I have been transformed by rape. Not only am I irreparably damaged, but I have become an embodiment of others' fear; a constant reminder that the worst could happen to them, too.

In this context, I am forced to ask, what kind of healing or survival is possible when rape is cast as the most extreme form of violation, an irreparable devastation, a permanent inscription on the body, the mind and the soul?

In trying to answer this, I reflect on how my sexuality (and personhood) was imbued with rape long before a man dragged me into those bushes. It is impossible for me to untangle my fear of rape from the "normative" shame I have always felt about being a sexual being. I have been configured, through both explicit tellings and silences, as an object of desire and not a subject who desires. Over and over, I learnt that my sexuality was something uncomfortable, even dangerous. In moments when I questioned my propensity for desire, the words 'whore' and 'slut' were levelled at me, sometimes from the mouths of others, sometimes from my own subconscious. Increasingly, I tried not to think about my sexuality. I definitely did not talk about it.

I was assured in this way of being, by the silent discomfort of my female friends and the absence of any discussion about female desire in the spaces I occupied. But perhaps most powerfully, I was assured by the continual connection made between "inappropriate" expressions of female desire (short skirts, flirting, drinking too much) and instances of sexual violence. The answer was clear: my shame was protective and if I was ashamed, I could keep myself safe. Therefore, I should remain ashamed.

Now, in what feels like far too late down the line, I am able to see how these deep feelings of shame have been central not only in constituting me as "woman," but as "white woman." In the process of unpacking my own violation, my attention moved to the violation of others around me. I observed the repeated representation of young, poor black womxn. It is no coincidence that the bodies most frequently violated are those of black womxn. It is also no coincidence that these instances of violence are strewn all over the media, unconcernedly pouring out gory details of the specific ways in which womxns' bodies have been violated. Constituted by hundreds of years of institutionalised racism, black womxn are simultaneously "unrapable" and inevitably raped. As Pumla Dineo Gqola so eloquently writes, "Making Black women impossible to rape does not mean making them safe against rape. It means quite the opposite: that Black women are safe to rape, that raping them does not count as harm and is therefore permissible."[51] Alongside this denial of harm, the constant reproduction of violated black bodies tells us that this type of violation is inevitable, unpreventable, and even mundane.

Through the dehumanisation of black womxn, my white body emerges as separate from this violence. For a long time, I was able to feel safe as I equated victimisation with blackness. My colonial ancestors would be pleased. They ultimately succeeded in constructing whiteness as "morally and sexually, not only racially, distinct from those regarded as belonging to other groups."[52]

But this racist sexualisation, and sexualised racism, keeps none of us safe. It strips us of our ability to identify with womxn who have experienced extreme forms of trauma and leads us to shame them, thereby confirming, for both ourselves and them, that rape is truly the worst thing that can happen. We are therefore all trapped in an endless cycle of shame, horror and violation.

For me, untangling and re-tangling my rape with my sexuality and race has been a starting point for reconstituting myself. In making explicit the layers of violence and violation, it is simultaneously more complex and also easier to read my experience. While this process has opened up many possibilities for despair, pain, anger and fear, it has also opened up space for hope and love – of myself and others. I use this love and hope to keep treading water and to continue to challenge racism, sexism, homophobia, and other forms of injustice. I fear that I am not done drowning, but neither am I done fighting to stay above the water.

Rebecca Helman is a PhD candidate at the University of South Africa. Her PhD, entitled *Post-Rape Subjectivities*, examines the ways in which rape survivours are able to (re)constitute their subjectivities amidst the discursive and material politics of sexual violence in South Africa. Rebecca is a researcher at UNISA's Institute for Social and Health Sciences and the South African Medical Research Council-UNISA's Violence Injury and Peace Unit.

FEMINISM AND SOCIETY: THE CULTURE OF OUR TIMES

FROM WOMEN TO 'GIRLS': LENA DUNHAM AS A NASTY WOMAN?

Stella Viljoen

When we march for change in society, the exact incentive behind our convictions is often informed by the soft politics of popular culture. We watch television, read magazines and use social media that impact our moral imagination and shape our sense of what the world ought to be like. Having a reality television star voted into office in the USA raises the question of whether we are paying enough attention to the precise ideologies that we encounter during our leisure time. Feminism, too, is shaped by popular mythologies that require careful disentangling so that we can discern what exactly they are teaching us.

In the mid-1970s, Laurie Simmons produced a series of photographs of miniaturised domestic interiors, first in black and white and later in colour. The close-up photographs of detailed bathrooms and sitting rooms that were initially surrealistically empty, later included a housewife doll poised over the kitchen table or sitting on the sofa. Simmons gained iconic status as a feminist artist and was included in "The Pictures Generation," a 2009 group show at the Museum of Modern Art in New York that included Cindy Sherman, Louise Lawler and Barbara Kruger. Simmons' work was considered feminist because of the way it articulated the strongly gendered nature of dolls and dollhouses as part of the subtle and not so subtle socialisation of children. Surely girls should be encouraged to live and dream beyond the "home," and surely boys should feel invested in family and domestic life? This simple logic, extended by second-wave feminism into the more political terrain of sexual liberty, was one I intuitively identified with. Equality was the central goal of this belief system, but like most forms of activism, I sensed an idealism at its heart, one that hoped to make the world a kinder, nicer place for men and women.

Skipping over third-wave feminism, and fast forwarding 40 years, Simmons' daughter, Lena Dunham, produced a semi-autobiographic short film called *Tiny Furniture* (2010) which eventually led to a television programme of almost cult status called *Girls* (HBO, 2012–2017). Dunham is the writer and director, and also stars as the main character, Hannah – a deeply self-involved 20-something who is supposedly trying to become a writer. When we meet her in the pilot episode, Hannah, an only child, is having dinner with her parents in a New York restaurant. They inform her that they will be cutting her allowance because she has been mooching off them long enough. They would like her to gain some independence and make her own way in the world. She is horrified and responds with whiney self-justification. She has no sense of responsibility or dignity, but is endearing and funny for this very reason, and the viewer cannot help but laugh at her unashamed attempt to manipulate, especially her father. It is a brilliant piece of filmic drama, arresting because of the paired down aesthetic. Hannah's parents are dowdy, the restaurant is dour, and the dialogue is awkward and honest. Is this even New York, the glitzy location for *Sex and the City* and *Gossip Girl*? Most startling is Hannah herself, who is far too "real"-looking to be a television star. From her hair colour to her body shape and posture, she is the very antithesis of a Hollywood lead. That's why we love her, and that's why the show is "feminist"...I think. This act of realism is no small thing. Hannah is a flawed anti-hero in the style of Willy Loman, who is also aspirational because of her honesty, wit, intelligence and loyalty as a character. She is more "real," complex and contradictory, than any other television character I have seen and that doesn't only include women characters – especially significant because of the superficiality and predictability of so many female characters on television.

But, the narrative is tremendously occupied with the sexcapades of Hannah and the other eponymous girls, to the extent that one feels the plot is driven forward by sex more than any other narrative device. This seems to be the most explicit site of Hannah's power as a woman, her sexual authority over her body. But the irony is that since so much of the story line revolves around who is sleeping with whom and how, women are defined, in literal and figurative ways, in terms of our sexuality, our bodily subjectivity. This is especially frustrating when Hannah treats her body so unkindly by sleeping with men who disrespect her, and brandishing this ability like it is a political right. She can sleep with whomever she wants to and therefore, if she chooses to disrespect herself by sleeping with a misogynist, this is her good right. Of course, this consequence of sexual empowerment rings true. But what does not, is that her willingness to sleep with men whom she knows will mistreat her is a feminist act. This is never stated explicitly, but the message is subtly communicated through the inordinate repetitions of a plot in which Hannah chooses to sleep with one jerk after another, only to be disregarded by them. Her feminist act is lost on the men whom she sleeps with, and whom the narrative casts in negative terms. Where is the idealism and political hopefulness I'm looking for out of feminist activism? Adding to the complexity of the plot, is the fact that all of the girls, Hannah included, actually desire a long-term mate. They are looking for love and not just sex, which calls into question the actual cynicism of the text. Is this not merely romance disguised as nihilism?

Girls is not alone in espousing this particular strain of post-feminism. Programmes like *Fleabag* and *Broad City* communicate something similar, as does stand-up comedian Amy Schumer. The protagonists of all are sharp, focused, funny women who represent incisive observations about the contradictions of modern womanhood. But they also merely replace one over-sexed subjectivity with another. I do not doubt their commitment to the cause or their status as feminists – Dunham has, for instance, started a critical and insightful online feminist newsletter with fellow *Girls* writer Jennifer Konner called 'Lenny Letter' – but I cannot help but feel that their hermeneutic of patriarchy is slightly different from mine. For me, and this may be a naïve telling, hegemony is defined in Marxist terms as willing submission to a dominant ideology in the service of a ruling class. In the patriarchal imaginary, women (and other subjected groupings) are encouraged to assume the kind of empowerment that is in fact fictive, a ruse, not real. True feminist counter-cinema is realist because it reveals the discrepancy between appearance and reality. It unmasks the cracks in a politics that is more pretence than radical provocation to change. Feminism is not feminist if it maintains the status quo.

Laurie Simmons' interior tableaus are so beautiful and inviting that they almost seem to endorse femininity-as-domesticity. But, they are just cloying enough to warn the viewer of this trap. In this way, they are truly feminist in the old-school sense, while still retaining an ambiguity. Dunham's *Girls*, in a sense, does the opposite. It upholds feminist sexual freedom as its confederate war flag, but interpolates the viewer into a sense of complacency about the expression of their agency. Hannah as character is a feminist act of fiction because she represents an objection to the glamorised, taught femininities on offer on television. She is a cry for normalcy in the very best sense. But, the programme as text does not invoke change, it does not point to what is wrong with the world. In fact, it normalises and glamorises what is wrong with the world. As Dunham develops as writer and director (and her doppelgänger, Hannah, enters into motherhood) I hope she remembers the activism of her mother that revealed patriarchy in such startling ways. Simmons' interiors also taught me, as a South African, something about the relationship between patriarchy and capitalism, the globalised, bourgeois dreams I was schooled in, since girlhood. Because politics is not just about whom you march for, but also about what television programmes you watch, I think it is important to critically evaluate the former and the latter. Without wanting to patronise an artist whom I deeply respect, I think Dunham is just the person to point a next generation toward the core conviction of feminism, that all deserve to be treated with dignity. Like the placard from the Women's March, my cry to her and her compatriots is, "Grab 'em by the patriarchy!"

Stella Viljoen is an associate professor in the Department of Visual Arts at the University of Stellenbosch, where she teaches Visual Studies. Her research is concerned with how so-called low- and highbrow cultures interact and imitate each other. Stella is currently documenting the rise of men's magazines in South Africa.

DOUBLE STIGMAS

Layla Al-Zubaidi

There are so many images and slogans from the global Women's Marches across the world that touched me, made me cheer, or laugh out loud. But one picture struck me in particular and it had an entirely different effect. Conflicting thoughts swirling around my head, I ended up with only questions and no answers. At the Women's March in Berlin, a woman wearing a US flag as a headscarf holds the poster, "OUR BODIES. OUR MINDS. OUR POWER."

She looks young and, by society's standards, pretty. Plucked eyebrows, bright red lipstick. Self-confident smile. An aura of female pride. The perfect, almost air-brushed human embodiment of American artist Shepard Fairey's iconic "We the People" poster held up next to her – a woman wearing a hijab patterned with stars and stripes calling upon the American people to overcome their fear.[53]

The unambiguous wording of the poster contrasts the mysteries of her identity. Who is she and what is her story? Is she really a believer, wearing a headscarf in everyday life? Or could it be a one-off show only, in solidarity with Muslim women? Muslim women, who in Trump's America carry a double stigma: as members of a gender whose pussies are up for grabbing, and as adherents to a faith that must be monitored, controlled, racially profiled, gagged, and if possible, kept out of sight and beyond the country's borders.

Why do I need to know her story, anyway? Would I dwell on the picture and poster for so long if her head wasn't covered, in a flag-slash-headscarf? Let's assume she is a Muslim German of migrant background, born in, or someone who grew up in, Germany. A country that only recently woke from its slumber, a decades-long denial of not wanting to call itself an immigrant society, to the fact that its population has changed. As in America, the stakes are high. With every progressive awakening, there comes a backlash. On the back of the "refugee crisis," a right-wing party and ally of Trump, Le Pen and Wilders, comfortably rode into national parliament for the first time after the end of World War II, and now forms its third biggest party. Even if the party will not repeat this success in the coming elections, as some optimists predict, it has achieved its damaging goal: the dams are broken; racism is socially acceptable again. Ten years ago, whispers such as "Muslims are bloodthirsty" or "Refugees are filth" were exchanged amongst fuming nationalists, pounding their fists on beer tables, not taken seriously by anyone. Today, it is dentists, economy professors, and school principals in suits and ties who shout "Let them drown in the sea!" through loudspeakers in town squares and sports stadiums. "Finally you may say what you think!" they exclaim, cheered by thousands. This crowd, that has never visibly cared for women, has now declared itself to be their sole custodian.

At the centre of the hatred are young, Muslim men who beat "their" wives and force "their" sisters to wear the hijab, and grope "our" girls. It is women's bodies, though, who serve as the sounding board. Those who, like me, know Germany's towns and streets from childhood, can feel it in the air. Something has changed. It is the veiled women on whom the stares rest in the subway and busses, tangible disgust on some faces. It is women in headscarves who have to fight at the courts for their right to remain in public service or work as teachers. The patronising pity once reserved for women who openly show their Muslimness has been replaced by something else. Men are feared, women are punished. The Muslim woman is not just a victim of patriarchy anymore. She is complicit in the crime.

On these grounds, I admire the unknown woman in the picture.

OUR BODIES, she says: I show my identity openly, and I defy the disadvantages that come with wearing a sign of a religion that is vilified and demonised. It was me who decided to don the hijab, as an expression of my faith and my religious duties.

OUR MINDS, she says: I don't want to be judged by what is on my head, but by what is in my head. My identity is not singular. I am a woman, a Muslim, a German, a citizen, a voter, all at the same time. I do not subscribe to the sexual objectification of women in mainstream culture and the media.

OUR POWER, she says: I am a feminist, and I don't bow down to the Eurocentrist idea that feminism needs to be the same everywhere. I defy Western generalisations about Muslim women as suppressed and passive victims. I resist the contempt for Muslims by some of Germany's most prominent feminists. For me, feminism and Islam are not at odds with one another. Islam does not confine me. See, I'm out here, mingling with gays and lesbians, Christians, Jews and atheists, protesting, expressing myself, affirming my convictions.

As a critique of both Trump's misogyny and Islamophobia, Shepard Fairey's image is an entirely laudable attempt. A national flag and a headscarf put together: Two pieces of simple fabric, and at the same time, two of the most powerful symbols of our time. Not pitted against each other, but combined. So why do I feel a sense of obliteration?

Maybe because I'm not American? My family's history and that of many of my friends are the human collateral of America's great democracy. The support for "stable" Arab dictatorships, the "surgical"

bombs and drones accidentally dropped on civilian targets, the double standards towards human rights at home and abroad. The half-hearted support for democratic opposition forces, including many women, first encouraged, then dropped and left alone to be preyed upon, jailed or ejected into a life of exile with scarred bodies and minds.

I wonder when the hijab became the dominant symbol for Islam, and for Muslim women? I am a Muslim woman by definition – I didn't choose my religion, I was born into it, and whether I practice or not, is not of public interest. I respect the choice of wearing a headscarf. It doesn't represent me, though, neither the many faces of Islam. In our family, my mother and I are the only women who still show our hair. All the other women have gradually veiled, either as a result of faith or fashion, in submission to social pressures, or because a popular television Imam in some rich Gulf country promises rewards. Or because they believe that the dark tunnel they find themselves thrown into today has come upon them as a God's punishment for the sin of having taken liberties in the past. At one point, for sure, I will be the very last one.

I believe in OUR bodies, OUR minds, OUR power. I respect that the American flag and the headscarf are sources of pride for some, even if not for me. I want to connect with all women, across all divides. I want more than Trump, to unite us. I want to be proud and to belong. Beyond nationality. Beyond religion. I don't have answers as to how we achieve this. I have just the simple wish to resist the rigid association of certain connotations with symbols of power.

Layla Al-Zubaidi is the director of Heinrich Böll Foundation's Southern Africa Office in Cape Town, South Africa. She was born in Germany to Iraqi and Syrian parents. She studied Social Anthropology in Germany and the United States, and specialises in human rights, women's rights, media and freedom of expression. Layla's published works include: *Anywhere but Now: Landscapes of Belonging in the Eastern Mediterranean* (HBF), *Unmaking Power: Democratic Transition in the Middle East* (Routledge), and *Writing Revolution: The Voices from Tunis to Damascus* (IB Tauris), which won the UK PEN award. The US edition (titled *Diaries of an Unfinished Revolution: Voices from Tunis to Damascus*) was published by Penguin. Her article on Syria's creative uprising appeared in the *London Review of Books*.

THOSE (NOT) ABLE TO BE BURNT

Melanie Judge

Women are burnt – across diverse locations, for different reasons, in both metaphorical and material ways.

At the United States Women's March against the election of Donald Trump as president, a protester held a poster with the words, "We are the granddaughters of the witches you weren't able to burn."

These words fold the then into the *now*, drawing a line from present-day "granddaughters" – as the living legacies of women's survival – to an ever-present "you," representing the continued smiting of women. Making these spatial and temporal connections is not to suggest that the experience of being a woman, or what constitutes womanhood for that matter, is, or has ever been, unified, singular or shared. Yet, to conjure such connections across the ages, reveals the resiliencies of gendered liveability across time, space and place. It is perhaps also an expression of the desire for feminist solidarities – through the act of remembering in the face of contemporary injustices.

WE ARE THE GRAND-DAUGHTERS OF THE WITCHES YOU WEREN'T ABLE TO BURN

119

But what does contemporary gender politics in the Global South, and in South Africa in particular, have to do with conjuring the history of the witch by those in the Global North? What does the figure of the witch call into consciousness about feminist politics across time and space? And can these fractured and fragmented strands of resistance be thought about alongside one another, in ways that illuminate, rather than obscure, the material differences that continue to thwart feminist alliances against multiple forms of injustice? How does remembering the witches of the past – and the enduring attempts to extinguish them – configure an imagined agent of radical change in the present?

Erasure and un-remembering are central to hetero-patriarchal nationalisms and the race, gender and class logics they underwrite. In this context, to position oneself in relation to lives unable to be lived, marks a refusal of dominant knowledges through which women's multiple histories are cast out of common consciousness. The witch-hunts that took place in early modern Europe had gender discipline at their core. It was the women who did not bow to social expectations and norms who were most readily accused of being witches, at a time when gender prescripts required them to be subordinated to men – as heads of house, Church and state. Women perceived as lusty, lively and independent were the main targets for attack. Older women no longer of childbearing potential, and younger women still to be moulded into feminine subordination, were particularly vulnerable. Moreover, women with the knowledge to be healers, thus threatening the burgeoning medical profession of men, were suppressed through witch-hunts. As a form of organised gender terror against the female population, such hunts were coordinated efforts to subject women to the political, religious and sexual dictates of patriarchal institutions and ideologies.

The *Malleus Maleficarum*, translated as "Hammer of Witches," was a treatise of the medieval Catholic Church endorsing the extermination of witches. It was the backbone narrative for the legal and theological justification of violence against women. Its essence, still reflected in contemporary patriarchal tropes, is captured in the assertion that, "When a woman thinks alone, she thinks evil." There are many women who think, and act, alone – in other words, outside of or against the dictates of domination. These women represent a necessary danger to the status quo and its sex, gender and race hegemonies, and continue to toil and trouble in contemporary times. Today, in certain regions of sub-Saharan Africa, women are still threatened with accusations of witchcraft and so persecuted. Recently in South Africa, a high-profile politician vilified his woman political opponents by calling them witches – in a country where women are still persecuted as witches even as Witchcraft itself is celebrated as a legitimate religion. The witch is the woman accused. Her persecution, as a form of gender correction, is a means to exert control over her sexuality, and over her social (childbearing) and economic (livelihood) production. Present-day witches include women who transgress sexual codes, who assert non-conforming gender identities, who survive violence and hold perpetrators to account, who call out racism against them and others, who refuse to assimilate into dominant cultures that seek to deny their own, who claim the right to health, education and land, who strike out against capitalist exploitation, and who refuse to separate demands for sexual freedom from that of racial and economic justice.

Women who defy systems of imposition that seek to diminish or even entirely destroy them, are, one might say, 'possessed' by the desire for another kind of social order. That possession is linked to the dispossession of the prospect of a life lived on one's own terms, and of the material and symbolic resources to render that life liveable.

There is a very real danger when feminist solidarities, and the past-present connections they draw on, are premised on erasing the differential experiences amongst women, given the plurality of our identities and social locations. Such erasures signify another kind of burning, or extinguishing, of the complex forms of oppression, and resistance to these, that women (en)counter. This, in turn, enables one set of demands for freedom (related, for example to gender) to become split off, even offset, against others (related to, for example, race and class).

> *"Sign: We can be burned*
> *We can be burned/shall I make the case for burning?*
> *The case for burning turns on what occurs when women are*
> *not burned"*
>
> – Howard Barker, *Slowly*[54]

In turning against the case for the burning of women, there is a call to those who are not (yet) at stake: those whose survivability as gendered beings is inextricably bound to the lives of those who are at stake. It is across such planes of radical re-identification that women who escape(d) the fires of violent exclusion might dare to imagine 'what occurs when women are not burned,' and so mobilise towards more equitable and inclusive futures.

Melanie Judge is a queer and feminist activist and scholar, and Adjunct Associate Professor in the Faculty of Law at the University of Cape Town. She is extensively involved in advocacy, law reform and research on gender and sexual rights, and LGBTIQ rights in particular, both locally and internationally. Melanie is author of *Blackwashing Homophobia: Violence and the Politics of Gender, Sexuality and Race*, and lead editor of *To Have and To Hold: The Making of Same-sex Marriage in South Africa*. Melanie serves as a trustee of GALA (South Africa's national LGBTIQ archive) and is the recipient of the Psychology and Social Change Award from Rhodes University in 2016.

NASTY CHINESE WOMEN SAY NO!

Riska Koopman

A few years back while doing preparatory readings to formulate my Masters research topic, I, like so many others, was bewildered by China's economic growth model. Specifically, I was interested in how the model is being marketed to Africa as an alternate path to answering the "dark continent's" wicked problems. The more I read, the more I wanted to know. So I spent a month in Shanghai, attending the New Development Bank's first Annual General Meeting and taking some courses at Fudan University. While sitting in meetings and lectures, walking in mammoth malls and breathtakingly beautiful Chinese gardens, I had one question: *"Where are the women?"* They were there, millions of them, but they were invisible in so many ways, side-lined by centuries of patriarchal rule. My Masters research started taking a more gendered approach, yet I was still unable to understand the socio-political context of economic growth and its impacts on womxn, until I moved to China for nine months. Literature on China's extraordinary economic rise, more often than not, leaves out the role womxn played and how they continued to be marginalised for the sake of economic growth and perceived social stability.

The Chinese Communist Party (CCP) has controlled women's pussies, wombs and pretty much everything else, since its inception 90 years ago. Under the one-child policy, the Ministry of Health estimates that there were 336 million forced abortions and up to 196 million men and women were sterilised.[55] Three in four Chinese were in favour of roughly 1,500 gender-biased abortions an hour, according to a 2008 study.[56]

The pussy-policing continues in China today. When the Chinese government realised it was contending with an aging population and low birth rates, the one-child policy was repealed. Women have subsequently been called to return home and have more babies[57].

Women, however, are mostly saying "hell no, we won't go," as they do not want the burden of a second child nor do they want to give up their already limited economic autonomy. I asked my Chinese colleagues what they thought about having two children and received a lukewarm, if mixed, response. Many said they simply could not afford it. One bereft colleague added that she could not even afford to have her only child live with her in the city.

The youngest of my colleagues dreamt of marrying an engineer and having as many children as he could afford. Her face fell when our slightly older male manager told her she had better hurry because her beauty was fading and so were her reproductive organs. I gasped, wanting to interject with "Excuse me, sir, did you know my mother got married at 40, Carrie Bradshaw well above that, and Janet Jackson only had her first baby yesterday (well, kinda)." But, of course, I did not say anything. You see, I've been schooled in respect, hierarchy, and how to get by in the deeply patriarchal society in which, according to my passport, I am now a resident.

My colleague is what is popularly known in China as a "left-over woman." These are typically single, professional women in their late 20s who are unmarried and childless. In 2007, the state began mocking women openly as left-over[58] if they remained unmarried after a certain age. Technically, however, due to gender-preference abortions, there are more single men than women in China, which anecdotally, is viewed as a growing problem. One to which women have once again been beckoned as the solution.

The campaign to focus obsessively on getting married, from what I can gather at a grassroots level, was hugely successful as my colleague probes me almost daily about dating-culture, marriage and child-bearing age in South Africa – rather than our fantastic weather, Nelson Mandela or the Big Five.

My colleague, her parents, and Chinese society at large, are overly concerned with both her ovaries and singleness. Every lunchtime, she pulls out the smallest hair curler known to humankind, creates soft curls around her jet black fringe, and pulls her lips a few times in a forward motion before applying a hideous shade of lipstick. The faffing continues, as she applies strange linear stickers of sorts to enlarge the lids of her eyes, meant to give her a more western look. Like clockwork, she ventures out to meet a potential husband in a speed date-like manner.

All of this must be so exhausting. The level of effort must be so tiresome, I think to myself. And there must be a point at which left-over women are catching on to the fact that all of this is played out, tired bullshit. The cemented idea of a paucity of life partners weighs heavily on both sexes in China, at times even more so for men, than I've experienced elsewhere. And within this context, social media platforms such as WeChat and the microblogging platform, Weibo, have become catalysts for feminist voices.

However, feminism is still in its infancy in China. The one-party state only opened up to the world about 30 years ago, which is why when people see me – a black South African woman – on the street, they literally lose their shit. Smartphones are whipped out and it's selfie time. Despite this, modern China still has a tight leash on the dissemination of information, because after all, knowledge is power. Statistically, women are the most vulnerable and powerless in most societies, and in China, with state-run media, men are entrenched at the helm of power.[59] One such institution of male power, the Politburo Executive Committee, exerts its power by any means to ensure that things remain this way.

University-educated and generally woke women in China are increasingly beginning to see the ways in which their roles have been shaped by and continue to be inhibited by oppressive strongmen state policies. These women are identifying as feminist. Their number, albeit small, is growing steadily. However, like most, my colleagues are not feminist. Most Chinese women shy away from identifying as feminist, as it is portrayed to be in direct opposition to the Confucian traits of a good daughter, good wife and good mother. Feminism is mostly a dirty word in China, reserved for lesbians, aggressive women, left-over women, agitators to the ruling party, and the like.

The word "feminist" only appeared as late as 2012, in the headline of a Chinese newspaper. Since then, it has featured an estimated 350 times, routinely with negative connotations.[60] Instability, aggression, lack of empathy and an aversion to family life are the socially undesirable traits associated with feminists.

Taiwan's first female president, Tsai Ing-wen, instead of being celebrated, has been denigrated and defamed in China. Official state mouthpieces are quick to besmirch her, arguing that women like her in positions of political power are prone to take extremist positions.[61] This article was eventually pulled due to large public outcry – a small but powerful and growing testimony to the effectiveness of social mobilisation, even in authoritarian China.

The World Health Organization (WHO) estimates that one in three women worldwide has experienced either physical or sexual violence in their lifetime.[62] In China, public transport interchanges such as bus terminals and the subway are places where women are particularly vulnerable to sexual assault.[63] In 2012, on Valentine's Day, Li Maizi and Wie Tingting, both 23 at the time, staged what became popularly known as the Wounded Brides[64] public demonstration, which would set off an unforeseeable chain of events. The pair, dressed in blood stained wedding gowns, chanted slogans like "hitting is not intimacy" and "verbal abuse is not love" in a busy Beijing commercial area. They also shared anti-domestic violence pamphlets with passersby, who welcomed their protest. At the time of this protest, China had no laws protecting women against domestic abuse. It was (and continues to be) widely viewed as a "personal" matter between husband and wife.

The next event, entitled "Occupy the Men's Room," was largely inspired by the "Occupy Wall Street" movement, launched in Guangzhou. Li and Wei were joined by other feminist activists. The project sought to achieve equal wait times in public restrooms for both sexes, by increasing the size of public restrooms for women. The event was warmly welcomed and duplicated in other cities in China. The feminists addressed the National People's Congress (NCP) with a formal letter, advising them to propose legislation to improve restroom facilities for women.

The issue was later raised during the NCP's legislative sessions. Continuing the successful momentum, the young Chinese feminists, also worked to replicate their success in other areas of women's rights including employment and education discrimination, gender-based violence and the rights of sex workers.[65]

As a result of these demonstrations, five women were arrested on 6 April 2015 under the charge of "gathering crowds to disturb the public order." What would ensue not only catapulted these women to the global stratosphere along with their feminist cause, but sparked national debates about issues such as feminism, state policing and women's rights; and perhaps, most importantly, exposed the fragile masculinity of China's authoritative regime.

China's *Feminist Five* have become synonymous with recent protest demonstrations, state oppression and the country's growing feminist movement. They are Li Tingting, age 25; Zheng Churan, age 25; Wei Tingting, age 26; Wu Rongrong, age 30 and Wang Man, age 33. They were detained in various locations since 6 April 2015, and due to mounting global outcry both from official bodies and online communities, released on bail seven days later on 13 April 2015, from the Haidian Detention Center in Beijing.

At the time of their arrest, the *Feminist Five* were preparing for an International Women's Day event entitled "7 March Stick-On Project" to be held on 7 March 2012, in Beijing and Gaungzhou. During a raid of Li's apartment, police found stickers that she had prepared for the anti-sexual harassment rally. On International Women's Day 2015, while Chinese President Xi Jinping was in New York co-hosting a United

Nations Summit on women's rights marking the 20th anniversary of the Beijing World Conference on Women, local police had detained the five women for inciting crowds, picking quarrels and provoking trouble. The news spread quickly, both locally and internationally. In China, citizens were stunned by the extreme measures that the state had taken to curb the spread of the feminist message. Despite the "Big Brother" nature of the state and growing police presence, the women's arrest alarmed "netizens," a term often used to refer to China's very active internet users. WeChat groups were quickly created and #FeministFive trended on social media platforms like Weibo, as well as on those banned within China such as Twitter, Facebook and Instagram. The decision to arrest the (then) largely unknown women was aptly described as "the spark the Chinese government provided itself with for the creation of a powerful new symbol of feminist dissent against a patriarchal, authoritarian state."[66]

Perhaps for the first time, feminist conversations were taking place in society. If nothing else was gained by their arrests, the inkling that China's system is hard-wired to unfairly benefit men at the expense of women is a (small) battle won. The state's reaction to the *Feminist Five* and the swift move to link their protest motives to foreign forces set tongues wagging. Li argued that the state used them as five chickens to scare the monkeys, which in hindsight, compounded by even greater clampdowns on freedom of thought and expression (particularly online), was rather successful.

The *Feminist Five* represented a larger community of young feminist activists. After the success of the "Occupy the Men's Room" protests, they decided to cast their net wider and tackle a broader set of issues. Perhaps they had been hitting areas too close for comfort. Issues of education and employment discrimination therefore provided the women with more followers to hitch onto their bandwagon.

Sile argues that the *Feminist Five* personify that which is to be stymied by the state.[67] In the same article, Xiaoming, a Chinese feminist scholar, adds, "What they (the state) are most scared of, is the entry of citizen expression into the public sphere." She further notes, "These activists possess clear public interest demands, utilise creative approaches and evoke positive media reaction. They constitute a sustainable force of activism, and thus an uncontrollable one."[68]

The *Feminist Five* garnered support from governments and official bodies globally. Canada, Britain and the European Union asked the Chinese government to release the women, while feminist organisations in the USA, Japan, Korea, India and Hong Kong expressed support and disdain by staging their own protests.

The #MeToo movement started in the USA with widespread allegations against Harvey Weinstein, in true fourth-wave feminism style, the internet was set ablaze in fury, and the naming and shaming of others globally ensued. The awakening or rise of a feminist movement is blossoming in China, too. The state is literally shaking, trying to Ctrl+Alt+Delete the voices of Nasty Chinese Women. Netizens are increasingly hopping on global feminist and anti-violence movements such as the #MeToo campaign. Prominent Chinese men across industries, spanning from entertainment to higher education and development, have been called out. The hashtag has since been blocked, and a post tying the host of China's most widely watched show has been deleted, presumably by the state. Despite this, Chinese citizens are still engaging in online debates. Chinese feminists are being forced to leave the country and continue their advocacy work from outside China, and prominent scholars and activists like Leta Hong Fincher and Li Maizi (*Feminist Five* members) provide popular opinion and lectures in countries like America and the United Kingdom. Thus, the silencing of these womxn has become a difficult task for the watchdog state – with citizens being increasingly creative and brazen in their approaches to questioning patriarchy, male privilege and, by default, the Communist Party of China.

As has been the case with feminist efforts around the world, where there are visible displays of social mobilisation in the public domain at both national and international levels, it is not easy to dispel them. Thus, locating feminist mobilisation within embedded networks, locally, regionally and globally, promises longevity and greater impact. By broadening the scope of such networks, we can engage with more issues and reach a wider audience, and bring together diverse sectors of societies and nations to find common ground in the fight towards the attainment of our feminist objectives.

Riska Koopman is currently completing her Masters Degree in International Relations at the University of Stellenbosch, where she also obtained her Bachelor of Arts and Bachelor of Commerce Honours degrees. She is fascinated by the impact of China's economic rise on the African continent, and her thesis focuses on the impacts of China's foreign direct investment on the South African economy. Riska was awarded both the DAAD-NRF and BRICS scholarships in 2016. She has since moved back to South Africa to work as the Civil BRICS Project Coordinator, continuing to work on China-Africa socio-economic and political exchanges.

STUCK IN THE MARGINS: WOMEN IN PRISON IN AFRICA

Lillian Artz

In 1906, Mark Twain popularised the saying, "There are three kinds of lies: lies, damned lies, and statistics." Statistics are an interesting thing. The former Statistician-General (SG) of South Africa, Mr Pali Lehohla, responsible for official statistics like the Census, once said that "statistics are about people, places and possibilities, not about numbers" and that they play an important role in planning, monitoring, policy development and decision-making. Indeed, and agreed, statistics are pretty useful. As a researcher, I generate and use statistics as the basis of advocacy work and they are certainly handy in getting one's point across. They can also be misleading. We have all witnessed how statistics are "used" to try to shape, or distort, our perceptions about how "good" or "bad" things are going in the country. Take the statistic (the prevalence) of five percent of "something," by example. Some might think that's a lot of somethings – *as many as* five percent or up to five percent – or that the somethings are hardly worth worrying about – *only* five percent of a thing is not bad.

Yet statistics, which we all use at one point or another to drive a point home, can not only be misleading, but they rarely tell the real "people-stories" behind the numbers. Take, for example, those who live on the margins, like women in prison. Of the South African prison population, 3.5 percent are women. Only? Up to? Most conversations about women in prison (almost without fail) prefer to read this as *only* 3.5 percent, and therefore "hardly worth the concern given the unprecedented rates of men in prison." But that is over 4,000 women behind bars, new ones imprisoned every year, and others released. I often wonder, how many "Nasty Women," what "ideal" percentage of them, does it take to even bother being concerned about?

I have spent five years – since the publication of *Hard Time(s): Women's Pathways to Crime and Incarceration* (2012) – jostling for spaces nationally and regionally to familiarise, enlighten and genuinely engage policy makers and prison reform advocates about the impact of imprisonment on "vulnerable people" in prison. I have been cautioned not to refer to this a "feminist advocacy" or to promote it as "feminist research," as this seemingly discredits what would be an otherwise credible position. I not only refer to women, but to other "vulnerable groups" in prison as well: children, the mentally ill, persons with intellectual and physical disabilities, victims of lifelong sexual, domestic or state-sanctioned violence, persons with addictions, the elderly, orphaned, abandoned and homeless children, HIV-positive persons denied of anti-retroviral medication (ARVs) and those with chronic illnesses, not to mention refugees, economic migrants, asylum seekers and internally displaced persons. People at the margins, and on the fringe, of mainstream prisoner human rights efforts.

Research, and other stories of women in prison in Africa, remains scarce and discrete, and for some, hardly worth advocating for given the "small numbers." Patching together the few sources available on women's incarceration, we know that women in Africa are prosecuted for a range of "offences" based on gender, sexuality, entrenched poverty, sex outside of marriage, obtaining abortions, HIV transmission, same-sex relationships,[69] "witchcraft,"[70] adultery (even after a reported rape), livestock and produce theft, and the inability to pose bail or fines (resulting in high rates of pre-trial detention).[71] Arbitrary detention and the lack of any legal representation compound already deep inequalities in the imprisonment of African women.[72] Even our local, South African, data leaves much to be desired. The Annual Report of the Department of Correctional Services (DCS) in 2015/16 reported that of the 161,984 offenders in South African prisons, 4,193 are women, a five percent increase from previous year (n=3915) and an 18 percent increase from three years earlier (n=3380 in 2012/13) – a signal that the imprisonment of women will not soon find relief. The DCS also reported (in 2013/14) that women are most likely to be sentenced for "economically related" (45 percent) offences.[73] That's *almost* half. There is no other "official" South African data on women in prison. That's it. How many there are, and what they are in for.

Small scale, prison-specific studies have gone some way towards providing a picture of women in prison, their pathways to imprisonment, and their experiences within and after prison.[74] Put together, these studies reveal the complex lives of women in prison: the average South African female offender is in her mid-to-late thirties, is most likely to be single or divorced, has children (over 75 percent do), is very unlikely to have completed secondary school, had their first child between the ages of 16-19 years old, and was incarcerated for the first time. South African women prisoners are also much less likely to be serial offenders or recidivists, and their age of first convictions is about 10 years older than that of men. Almost half of South African women in prison reported having had, or have, a male member of the family in prison, of which male siblings made up a third of these incarcerations. That's a lot, and gives some indication that the lived realities of women who end up in prison, were "not all right".

And, then there are the conditions that women face when in prison ...

The conditions that women face in prison are horrific. In 2015, Constitutional Court Judge Edwin Cameron, released a report on the conditions of Pollsmoor "Women's Centre" (a bizarre euphemism used by DCS to mean "prison," as though it were a community or recreational hub). Here, he describes the conditions in which women in South African prisons are detained:

> The remand cell visited was in as poor a condition as the male remand cells. 94 women were crowded into a poorly aerated room. The women shared beds or slept on the floor on thin mattresses. The mattresses were stinking. There was no working toilet, a clogged sink drain, and only cold water. They showed us tattered and torn sheets and blankets, which were infested with lice. They noted that the cell was also infested with cockroaches. Finally, the women complained that as remand detainees they were not afforded library books or magazines to read, fights often broke out. They attribute this to extreme boredom.[75]

A year later, the Public Service Commission conducted a similar investigation into the condition of cells in South African prisons, which they found to be "untenable," "highly congested and cluttered" and "untidy and not fit for human habitation,"[76] and that the environment was unhygienic and posed a serious health risk since the cells have open toilets often filthy due to overcrowding.[77] Yet, questions from sceptics persist: Why should we be concerned with women in prison when so many women who have not committed crimes live in uninhabitable conditions? They are less than four percent of the South African prison population, what about the *men who* make up 96 percent of the prison population? Why should we put funding towards so few, when so many others are in need? Surely whatever reforms we advocate for the general population (men), will also benefit women?

Because, women are "just" 3.5 percent, right?

Let's put this into perspective: the global, the regional, and the local. More than 10.35 *million* people are held in penal institutions throughout the world according to the latest edition of the World Prison Population List (WPPL), an annual review researched and compiled by Roy Walmsley.[78] 10.35 million people. This is ("only") 0.0014 percent of the world's population. The WPPL further reports that since the year 2000, the world prison population total has grown by almost 20 percent and the total female prison population has increased by a staggering 50 percent (the equivalent figure for the male prison population is 18 percent). In Africa, the rate of incarceration is reported to have increased by 22.6 percent during this same period. And globally, 700,000 women and girls are held in prisons throughout the world,[79] either as pre-trial detainees/remand prisoners, or having been convicted and sentenced.

But is that enough? Do we need more?

These trends in women's incarceration continue to be dismissed as "only affecting a few." It takes me back to one of my first feminist criminology texts by Adelberg and Currie, *Too Few to Count: Canadian Women in Conflict with the Law* (1987), a text that opened my eyes to the significance of feminist theory, the absolute (versus just an "ideological") need for feminist research, and a text which remains in my arsenal of literature on "women, crime and social control." Yet, 30-something years later, and with the global average rate of women's incarceration increasing by 50 percent in half this time, there are still "too few to count;" still too few to bat an eye at. We are talking about people who, prior to incarceration, already lived on the margins of society with poor health and health care access. Women who spent lifetimes exposed to sexual violence and domestic abuse, over and over, by people they should have been able to trust: parents, caregivers, neighbours, teachers, partners. Women, from our own communities, with drug and alcohol addictions, undiagnosed or untreated mental health issues, chronic health conditions, who lost parents and children to preventable diseases and violence, who lived in poverty and who once lived next to you. Women who have children that were taken away after they were sentenced, who are now lost in the system, that do not ever visit or cannot be found.

What if I told you that some of these women were as fallible, human and just like us, and got in with the wrong crowd, fell under the influence of lovers and family members, or made spectacularly poor choices under equally diabolical structural conditions?

What if I told you that I have spoken to women in prison who were 60-something ex-librarians and small business book-keepers, mothers protecting themselves and their children from dangerously abusive partners, women who did ask for help and who were disregarded and dismissed?

What if I told you that I met women who pulled themselves out of poverty through "shading dealings" in their determination to build a better – less violent, less impoverished, less burdened – future for their children, and women who were sexually assaulted as toddlers, and again as children, and again as adolescents, and again by their "intimate partners"?

Would you give a shit then?

Lillian Artz is an Associate Professor and Director of the Gender, Health and Justice Research Unit (GHJRU) in the Faculty of Health Sciences, University of Cape Town. She has published widely on domestic violence, sexual offences, incarcerated women and women's rights to freedom and security in Africa. Her current work includes research on female and other key populations in prisons and psychiatric settings, the epidemiology and prevalence of child sexual abuse, exposure to coercive sexual experiences amongst HIV testing populations, torture prevention in places of detention, as well as the medico-legal management of sexual and other forms of gender-based violence in conflict-affected, post-conflict and transitional African states. Lillian has worked as a technical consultant to a wide range of national human rights institutions, international development agencies and justice systems in Southern, Central and East Africa.

A WOMAN'S PLACE IS IN THE RESISTANCE

Juliana Claassens

Scrolling through all the fabulous signs featured at the Women's Marches, I found myself unable to decide which one to reflect upon for this Nasty Women project. Just too many good ones! This indecision is evident in the fact that I will cheat (being a nasty woman after all!) and will refer to more than one. But hopefully it will be clear that they all are connected.

The first sign that caught my attention is the one with Princess Leia on it that proclaims that "a woman's place is in the resistance." My attraction to this sign is not so much that I am a Star Wars fan, but that I have been writing about resistance in the biblical traditions for a long time and can completely identify with this assertion. In many ways, my own life can be said to be a story of resistance. I was one of the first female theological students at the University of Stellenbosch and am now the second female professor in the Faculty of Theology's 159 year history (a journey that I have reflected on in a recent monograph, *Claiming Her Dignity: Female Resistance in the Old Testament*).[80]

In some sense, all the women showing up for the recent Women's Marches would agree with the claim that "a woman's place is in the resistance." From the women in suffragette costumes who claimed that what they are fighting is the "Same shit. Different century." And the young girl who implores Donald Trump to stop building walls and to instead cultivate kindness. And the many old women who in no uncertain terms proclaim that they cannot believe that they still must be fighting this &**$66)&&!!

These signs show us how the Women's Marches brought together old and young, men and women, immigrants and citizens, gay and straight, white and black, to collectively say "No!" to a life-denying culture that has permeated everything the new US administration has done in the past months. But a deeper reason why these Women's Marches struck such a chord is the realisation that many women all around the world know all too well. Things have changed, but too much still remains the same. This is evident from the fact that many of us are still fighting colleagues at work who have trouble seeing us as equals; that we still find women being objectified and trivialised in the media as well as in society at large; that too many women globally continue to be excluded from educational opportunities or economic empowerment; that it is still not safe to walk around alone after dark, or sometimes even in broad daylight.

In her book on the politics of protest, *Notes Toward a Performative Theory of Assembly*, Judith Butler writes that "when bodies gather as they do to express their indignation and to enact their plural existence in a public space, they are also making broader demands: they are demanding to be recognised, to be valued, they are exercising a right to appear, to exercise freedom, and they are demanding a livable life."[81] The women at the marches were making this claim, both individually and collectively. "We are here!" "We deserve to be recognised and more importantly, to be valued." "We demand a liveable life!"

For Butler, as was also evident in the Women's Marches, it is important that this protest brings together various groups who find themselves in a state of precarity, who are, in Butler's words, struggling "in, from and against precarity." For Butler, precarity is a common denominator that "brings together women, queers, transgender people, the poor, the differently-abled, and the stateless but also religious and racial minorities."[82] She argues that bodies should be in alliance, that individuals and groups should work together to resist precarity and should form links across diversity.[83]

This said, for me the sign that best captures Butler's call to solidarity amongst groups who find themselves in situations of precarity after Donald Trump was elected President of the USA, is the advertisement for the Washington DC Women's March (21 January 2017) that shows multiple intertwined hands stretching out, demanding change. This call to solidarity reflects for me something of what Hillary Clinton's campaign slogan (and yes, as my brother has rightly pointed out, I, together with many others, have trouble accepting that she has lost the election!!) said so well: "Stronger together." Even though she lost the election, it is still true that we need to stand together across that which divides us.

Butler makes the important observation that the ultimate goal of any form of resistance, both individual and collective, should be the desire to live a good life, not just for ourselves, but also for others.[84] Her key argument is that resistance should be "embodied," and that it should be "plural," dedicated to "a new way of life, a more liveable life."[85] In this way, "acts of resistance will say no to one way of life at the same time that they say yes to another."[86]

The hundreds of thousands of women who showed up for the Women's Marches call upon us to claim our place in the resistance. To say out loud: "As long as we live, we will continue to resist until every woman has the basic human right to live free, unencumbered, fulfilled lives."

Juliana Claassens is Professor in Old Testament at the Faculty of Theology at the University of Stellenbosch. Before moving back to teach at her alma mater, she spent 13 years in the USA, during which time she studied at Princeton Theological Seminar and taught in Greenbay, WI, Richmond, VA and Washington DC. Her most recent book, *Claiming Dignity: Female Resistance in the Old Testament* was published with Liturgical Press (2016). She is also author of *Mourner, Mother, Midwife: Reimagining God's Liberating Presence* (Westminster John Knox, 2012) and *The God who Provides: Biblical Images of Divine Nourishment* (Abingdon, 2004). Juliana is also the Director of the Gender Unit at the Faculty of Theology that seeks to offer a creative space for conducting interdisciplinary research on an intersectional understanding of gender.

THE EMBODIMENT OF
OUR STRENGTH

Ellen DB Riggle

When I see this picture, it reminds me that this "nastiness" did not just begin, and will not just end. This is a long-term commitment to being strong and supporting the strength of others, especially women. The 2017 Women's Marches were a show of strength. Many of the signs referenced strength in a variety of definitions, illustrations and metaphor. But, what does strength mean, and how can we define it for ourselves, as a resource for moving forward?

Strength in numbers. The conventional wisdom is that numbers matter. A mass protest draws attention and conveys a formidable force. A force to be reckoned with, which translates into power and influence. The ability to organise a group is a strength. In the case of the Women's Marches moving forward, and the representation of women's interests (indeed, the interests of all), it will be necessary to act

en mass. What was especially impressive, and left an impression, was the worldwide organisation of the Women's Marches, a transnational strength in numbers. This recognition of our common interests and interdependencies is vital to amassing support.

Strength in visibility. Women are supposed to be quiet, invisible. A few women gathered may draw attention; a mass of women intends to be seen and heard. An amassing of women refuses to be silenced, conveying the power of our presence. Women's visibility and voice is a source of strength. One of the challenges of the Women's Marches moving forward will be to continue to be visible and heard in thousands of locales. Effective visibility inspires others, even those who must remain invisible and silent. Visibility claims the public space and creates a public voice.

Strength in diversity. Diversity has become in many ways an overused word, rendering it a cliché. Women must break from the cliché and embrace the strength found in diversity of thought, of form, of inclusion. Diversity provides us with opportunities to learn, expand, grow, and move forward. The Women's Marches must continue the commitment to attracting and actively embodying diversity. Building coalitions of diverse peoples is a challenge and requires that we learn to be good, loyal allies. It is this strength that will keep the movement moving forward.

Strength in herstory. The Women's Marches are a continuation of a long history of action by women, on behalf of social justice and in pursuit of their own rights. The speakers and signs at the Women's March make clear linkages to those who have come before. The marches supporting women's suffrage in different parts of the world, and women's anti-pass protests in South Africa, are just two modern era examples of women coming together, using their strength to demand change and justice. These marches and protests, and the women who led them, inspire our current generation of women to take action. Those women and their courage laid the foundation for women now. Their strength still runs through the veins of women today, and they must be remembered and honoured.

Strength in muscle. Women are supposed to be weak, submissive, and able to be dominated. Muscle is a source of health, a symbol of agency and independence, a tool for activity. The building of muscle, the ability to move, must be supported for girls and women. Health, including reproductive health, must be a priority. This includes the strength that comes from clean water and fresh food. The Women's Marches must recognise and make environmental and economic justice a priority in order to support women's health, and global health. Healthcare must be a right, not a privilege.

Strength in non-conformity. Actively challenging the status quo, and its normatively gendered scripts and socialisation, is a source of strength. Non-conformity creates space for, and encourages, creativity. Our scripts must be actively re-written. The Women's Marches gave space to unleash creativity (which led to the signs in this book). Women's creative strengths have been honed by years of survival and necessity. This creativity must be nurtured to support continued active resistance. Creativity is necessary to writing new scripts that will look beyond and replace the patriarchy. Creativity is the basis of the responsible opposition becoming the responsible society.

Every woman, every person, has strengths. Strong women have always been called "Nasty Women." The Women's Marches need to encourage the discovery and development of each individual's strengths. We must empower women to recognise and embrace our own strengths as part of our authentic life. Strength must include the so-called "feminine." Strength must include compassion and empathy – the bases of our connections with others. Strength must include the discipline to be flexible – to see change as good and positive. Strength must include recognising and respecting the contributions of each woman, each person – even when those contributions look different from our own. The Women's Marches marked one point in time from which we move forward and embody our strengths to support our collective humanity.

Ellen DB Riggle was raised on a small farm in rural Indiana in the United States. She attended Purdue University and the University of Illinois. She is currently a Professor of Gender and Women's Studies and Political Science at the University of Kentucky and co-founded PrismResearch.org, dedicated to enhancing research on and contributing to the well-being of LGBTIQ individuals and communities.

ENDNOTES

Pussies Are Not For Grabbing!

1   *Nasty Women* Poem by Nina Mariah Donovan. [hellogiggles.com/lifestyle/19-year-old-woman-wrote-nasty-woman-poem-ashley-judd-womens-march/] (Accessed 5 August 2017).

2. Bartky S, 1977. *Towards a Phenomenology of Feminist Consciousness* in Vetterling-Bragging, M, Elliston, F and English, J (eds) *Feminism and Philosophy*, Totowa: Littlefield and Adams.

My Arms Are Tired of Holding This Sign

3   Nixon R, 2013. *Slow Violence and the Environmentalism of the Poor.* Harvard: Harvard University Press.

4. Monbiot G. "The Deep Story that Lies beneath Donald Trump's Triumph", *The Guardian*, 4 November 2016. [www.theguardian.com/commentisfree/2016/nov/14/neoliberalsim-donald-trump-george-monbiot](Accessed 15 May 2017)

5   Whips.

Nasty Women Run the World – Running for and from Public Office

6   Hillary R. Clinton, Concession Speech, 9 November 2016.

7   At the time of writing in 2017, as the appointment process is now well under way (June 2018).

8   Bohnet I, 2016. *What Works: Gender Equality by Design*, Cambridge: Harvard University Press.

9   Burrell B, 2012. "Practicing Politics: Female Political Scientists as Candidates for Elective Office", *Political Science and Politics*, 45(1): 83-86.

10 Frederick A, 2013. "Bringing Narrative In: Race-Gender Storytelling, Political Ambition, and Women's Paths to Public Office", *Journal of Women, Politics & Policy*, 34(2): 113-137.

11 Lawless J and Fox R, 2005. *It Takes A Candidate: Why Women Don't Run for Office*, New York: Cambridge University Press.

Don't Forget: White Women Voted for Trump

12 [http://www.telegraph.co.uk/women/politics/donald-trump-sexism-tracker-every-offensive-comment-in-one-place/]

13 [www.vox.com/policy-and-politics/2017/1/20/14061660/women-march-washington-vote-trump]

14 [www.theatlantic.com/magazine/archive/2017/10/the-first-white-president-ta-nehisi-coates/537909/]

15 [www.theguardian.com/us-news/2017/sep/25/white-women-husbands-voting]

16 [www.psychedinsanfrancisco.com/white-women-vote-trump/]

17 [www.teenvogue.com/story/womens-suffrage-leaders-left-out-black-women]

18 [www.colorlines.com/articles/why-im-skipping-womens-march-washington-opinion]

19 [www.newyorker.com/culture/jia-tolentino/the-somehow-controversial-womens-march-on-washington]

20 [www.colorlines.com/articles/police-shooting-justine-damond-ruszczyk-exposes-vicious-double-standard-opinion]

21 [everydayfeminism.com/2016/07/protect-white-womanhood/]

22 [www.colorlines.com/articles/emmett-till-was-lynched-day-1955-martin-luther-king-jr-told-world-about-his-dream-8-years]

23 [www.colorlines.com/articles/your-henrietta-lacks-reading-list]

Build Bridges Not Walls

24 The Department of Homeland Security provides the lower figure. The higher figure is that calculated by Democratic staffers at the Senate Committee on Homeland Security and Governmental Affairs, based on per-mile costs based on Trump's initial request for wall funding. Nixon R, 2017. "Border Wall Could Cost 3 Times Estimates, Senate Democrats' Report Says," *New York Times.* [www.nytimes.com/2017/04/18/us/politics/senate--democrats--border--wall--cost--trump.html?_r=0] (Accessed 18 April 2017)

25 Walker T, 2016 "For some, Donald Trump's dark border dreams are already a reality," *Independent.* [www.independent.co.uk/news/world/americas/donald-trump-border-wall-nogales-arizona-clinton-a7368831.html] (Accessed 20 October 2016).

26 Trump supporters are those whose identity politics are overwhelmingly shaped by whiteness and the sense of having been made downwardly mobile or isolated by globalisation; and who are of the perception that social policies favour African Americans, Hispanics, Muslims and migrants. They are over-represented in the rust belt, small white towns and white rural communities, and in many southern states. My thanks to Jeanne Laux for sharing her insights into the socio-spatial constitution of Trump's base.

27 In 2012, researchers found that "fully a third of US unauthorised immigrants in the workforce (33%) held service jobs such as janitor, childcare worker or cook, nearly double the share of US-born workers (17%) in those types of

occupations." Passel J and Cohn D, 2007. "Share of Unauthorised Immigrant Workers in Production, Construction Jobs Falls Since." *States Hospitality, Manufacturing and Construction are Top Industries*, Pew Research Center. March 2015, [www.pewhispanic.org/files/2015/03/2015-03-26_unauthorised-immigrants-passel-testimony_REPORT.pdf]

28 Merkel A, 2017. "Merkel: Building walls doesn't equal success," *CNN* Video, [www.cnn.com/videos/world/2017/05/25/angela-merkel-building-walls-nato-berlin-wall.cnn]

29 Kershner I, 2017. "Trump Cites Israel's 'Wall' as Model. The Analogy if Iffy," *New York Times*. [www.nytimes.com/2017/01/27/world/middleeast/trump-mexico-wall-israel-west-bank.html?_r=0] (Accessed 27 January 2017).

30 Notably absent among the "Muslim majority" countries excluded from the travel ban are those with which the Trump Organisation does business including Saudi Arabia, Lebanon, Turkey, the UAE, Egypt and Indonesia. The revised travel ban introduced in March 2017 also exempts Iraq, based on the Pentagon's argument that including Iraq in the first ban undermined relations with a country with which the US is currently engaged in the fight against Isis. As critics have noted, the country ban list bears little relationship to the actual incidence of terror attacks associated with these countries or the nationality of terrorists that have attacked Americans in the USA or abroad. Notably 15 of the 19 "9/11" hijackers were citizens of Saudi Arabia, exempted from Trump's travel ban.

31 Swaine J, 2017. "Trump breaks from Obama with crime crackdown and 'blue lives matter' protection," *The Guardian*. [www.theguardian.com/us-news/2017/feb/09/trump-criminal-justice-reform-police-protections-obama] (Accessed 10 February 2017).

32 Lebron C, 2017. "An Open Letter to the Editors of the *Journal of Political Philosophy*; or How Black Scholarship Matters, Too." [www.politicalphilosopher.net] (Accessed 24 May 2017).

33 Ross J and Lowery W, 2017. "Black Lives Matter switches to policy battles," *The Washington Post*. [www.pressreader.com/usa/the-washington-post/20170508/281513636065669] (Accessed 8 May 2017)

Haunting

34 [www.m.dailykos.com/stories/1641415]

35 [www.haltactiongroup.com/?cat=4]

36 [https://www.nytimes.com/2017/11/28/us/politics/donald-trump-tape.html]

Oh, No You Can't Go to Heaven In a Broke Down Car

37 Folk song commonly sung on the Cape Flats, Cape Town, South Africa.

38 A "purity promise" is a pledge made by young girls to not have sex until they are married.

39 They are, after all, only men.

40 Punishment and admonishing.

Diary of an Indian Woman

41 "Caste" refers to a classification system used amongst Hindus to rank different classes. Some are considered more superior than others.

Walking Tall, Walking Together

42 Putuma K, 2017 *Collective Amnesia* Cape Town: Uhlanga Press.

43 Shared by Khaya Dlanga on Twitter [www.twitter.com/khayadlanga/status/882142008768421888]

44 This incident was reported to my manager who began formal processes to arrange a meeting with the perpetrator and his line manager. He was ill, and his manager was not able to arrange a meeting to resolve his behaviour. This process of trying to arrange a meeting took several months, and before we were able to meet he passed away. I believe that in a workplace where sexual harassment was taken seriously, where it was not normalised and accepted, this meeting would have happened immediately.

45 Shared by girlsnrgorg on Instagram [www.instagram.com/p/BT-N201Ddnd/]

"I'm With Her"

46 "Vision and Mission," Women's March. [www.womensmarch.com/mission] (Accessed 15 July 2018).

To Womb It May Concern

47 Physical or intellectual pleasure, delight, or ecstasy.

48 Queer scholar, Judith Butler, writes in *Bodies That Matter. On the Discursive Limits of 'Sex'* (1993) about how we try and try again through endless iterations to embody norms. In the case of these particular Duracell Bunnies, they attempt to accomplish an oppressive form of heteromasculinity by attempted vanquishing of their sexual others.

Thoughts on Rape, Race and Reconstituting Subjectivity

49 I prefer to use the term "womxn" to refer to "all people who identify as femme, female, women, or trans" (Reddy D. 2016. *"It's a business doing pleasure*

with you:" *A case for the decriminalisation of sex work in South Africa* (Unpublished doctoral dissertation)), Haverford College, Pennsylvania: 8.

50   hooks b, 1984. *Feminist Theory: From the Margin to the Centre.* Boston: South End Press.

51   Gqola P, 2015. *Rape: A South African Nightmare*, Johannesburg: MFBooks: 4 -5.

52   Ratele K, 2009. "Sexuality as Constitutive of Whiteness in South Africa", NORA: *Nordic Journal of Feminist and Gender Research*, 17:3: 158-174.

Double Stigmas

53   Shepard Fairy designed three "We the People" women posters in the style of his "Hope" poster, which became the symbol of Barack Obama's campaign and electoral victory in 2008. Protesters used the women posters widely in the global Women's Marches against Donald Trump.

Those (Not) Able to be Burnt

54   Barker H, 2012. *Slowly: Hurts Given and Received.* London: Oberon Books.

Nasty Chinese Women Say NO!

55   Moore M, 2013. 336 million abortions under China's one-child policy. [www.telegraph.co.uk/news/worldnews/asia/china/9933468/336-million-abortions-under-Chinas-one-child-policy.html] (Accessed, 12 October 2017)

56.   Pew Research Centre. 2008. The Chinese celebrate their roaring economy, as they struggle with its costs. [www.pewglobal.org/2008/07/22/the-chinese-celebrate-their-roaring-economy-as-they-struggle-with-its-costs/] (Accessed 12 October 2017)

57   Jinghua Q, 2016. Return home and "Settle", Confucians tell women. www.sixthtone.com/news/745/Return%20Home%20and%20%E2%80%98Settle,%E2%80%99%20Confucians%20Tell%20Women] (Accessed 16 September 2017)

58   Fincher L, 2016. China's Feminist Five for Dissent Magazine Online. [www.dissentmagazine.org/article/china-feminist-five] (Accessed 4 October 2017)

59   Tatlow D, 2017. As China prepares for new top leaders, women are still shut out. [www.nytimes.com/2017/07/16/world/asia/china-women-communist-party.html] (Accessed 10 October 2017)

60   Jiawen Z, 2017. How internet prejudice threatens feminist progress. [www.sixthtone.com/news/2004/How%20Internet%20Prejudice%20Threatens%20Feminist%20Progress] (Accessed 24 September 2017)

61 Jiawen Z, 2017. How internet prejudice threatens feminist progress. [www.sixthtone.com/news/2004/How%20Internet%20Prejudice%20Threatens%20Feminist%20Progress] (Accessed 24 September 2017)

62 World Health Organization, November 2016. Violence against women. [www.who.int/mediacentre/factsheets/fs239/en/] (Accesssed 12 October 2017)

63 Lianzhang W, 2017. Throat-cutting molester arrested for attempted homicide. [www.sixthtone.com/news/1000828/throat-cutting-bus-molester-arrested-for-attempted-homicide] (10 October 2017)

64 Sile Z, 2015. The inspirational backstory of China's Feminist Five. Viewed foreignpolicy.com/2015/04/17/china-feminist-bail-interview-released-feminism-activist/] (3 October 2015)

65 Sile Z, 2015. The inspirational backstory of China's Feminist Five. Viewed, [foreignpolicy.com/2015/04/17/china-feminist-bail-interview-released-feminism-activist/] (3 October 2017)

66 Fincher L, 2016. China's Feminist Five for Dissent Magazine Online. [www.dissentmagazine.org/article/china-feminist-five] (4 October 2017)
    Sile Z, 2015. The inspirational backstory of China's Feminist Five. Viewed [foreignpolicy.com/2015/04/17/china-feminist-bail-interview-released-feminism-activist/] (3 October 2017)

68 Sile Z, 2015. The inspirational backstory of China's Feminist Five. Viewed [foreignpolicy.com/2015/04/17/china-feminist-bail-interview-released-feminism-activist/] (Accessed 3 October 2017)

Stuck in the Margins: Women in Prison in Africa

69 Todd–Gher J, 2014. "Policing Bodies, Punishing lives: The African Women's Protocol as a tool for resistance of illegitimate Criminalisation of Women's Sexualities and Reproduction," *African Human Rights Law Journal*, 14: 725- 756.

70 UNICEF, 2012. Children Accused of Witchcraft: An Anthropological Study of Contemporary Practices in Africa.

71 United Nations Office on Drugs and Crime. 2007. *Handbook of Basic Principles and Promising Practices on Alternatives to Imprisonment.* [www.unodc.org/pdf/criminal_justice/Handbook_of_Basic_Principles_and_Promising_Practices_on_Alternatives_to_Imprisonment.pdf] (Accessed, 14 March 2017).

72 Ackermann M, 2016. "Women in detention in Africa: A Review of the Literature". *Agenda: Empowering Women for Gender Equity*, 106: 80-91.

73 Department of Correctional Services, 2016. 2015/2016 *Annual Report*. South Africa: Department of Correctional Services.

74 Africa A, 2015. "Bad Girls to Good Women – Women Offenders' Narratives of Redemption". *Agenda*, 196(29): 120-128; Artz L, Hoffman-Wanderer Y and Moult K 2012. *Hard Time(s): Women's Pathways to Crime and Incarceration*. South Africa: UCT/European Union and the Office of the Presidency; Luyt W F M and du Preez N. 2010. "A Case Study of Female Incarceration in South Africa." *Acta Criminologica*. 23(3): 88-114; Haffejee S, Vetten L and Greyling M. 2005. "Exploring Violence in the Lives of Women and Girls Incarcerated at Three Prisons in Gauteng Province, South Africa." *Agenda*. 66: 40-47.

75 Cameron E, 2015. *Pollsmoor Correctional Centre – Remand Centre and Women's Centre*. Constitutional Court of South Africa Report: 25.

76 Public Service Commission, 2016. *Consolidated Report on Service Delivery Inspections Conducted in the Department of Correctional Services*. South Africa: Public Service Commission: 5.

77 Public Service Commission, 2016. *Consolidated Report on Service Delivery Inspections Conducted in the Department of Correctional Services*. South Africa: Public Service Commission: 10.

78 Walmsley R, 2016. *World Prison Population List*. Institute for Criminal Policy Research. University of London.

79 Walmsley R, 2015. *World Female Imprisonment List*. Institute for Criminal Policy Research. University of London.

A Woman's Place is in the Resistance

80 Claassens J, 2016. *Claiming Her Dignity: Female Resistance in the Old Testament*, Collegeville MN, Liturgical Press.

81 Butler J, 2015. *Notes Toward a Performative Theory of Assembly*, Cambridge: Harvard University Press: 26.

82 Butler J, 2015. *Notes Toward a Performative Theory of Assembly*, Cambridge: Harvard University Press: 122.

83 Butler J, 2015. *Notes Toward a Performative Theory of Assembly*, Cambridge: Harvard University Press: 58.

84 Butler J, 2015. *Notes Toward a Performative Theory of Assembly*, Cambridge: Harvard University Press: 67-68.

85 Butler J, 2015. *Notes Toward a Performative Theory of Assembly*, Cambridge: Harvard University Press: 203.

86 Butler J, 2015. *Notes Toward a Performative Theory of Assembly*, Cambridge: Harvard University Press: 217.